ChemBro

Embracing Beastmode to Beat Cancer

ChemBro

Embracing Beastmode to Beat Cancer

Adam Bernard

Advance Reviews of ChemBro

"Adam Bernard's journey through meeting and beating cancer is full of inspirational vignettes that tell the story of how perseverance and a zest for life are the keys to combatting anything. Adam's first-person anecdotes take us from the very beginning to the moments of success and celebration, showing how cancer didn't stand a chance when your will is strong. A relatable writer, his story can touch anyone facing adversity and also doubles as a strong nudge to anyone who shuns the importance of leading a healthy lifestyle. Adam B tells it like it is, and we're all made better because of it."

    – Kathy Iandoli, author and journalist

"A friend you didn't know has written a book for you that you didn't know you needed. I imagine that this book must be indispensable for anyone with testicular cancer, given that it's indispensable for everyone else. "

    – Homeboy Sandman, hip-hop artist

"Adam Bernard's ChemBro is an eye-opening, nerve-wracking and ultimately heartwarming hand-in-hand journey into one man's experience with chemotherapy and his impressive, inspirational recovery. The vulnerability Adam shows is only matched by his razor-sharp laser-precise wit and his masterful writing. Whether you or someone you know is going through the process, or you're interested in what balancing chemotherapy with an in-demand freelance music writing career and super-human CrossFit schedule entails, ChemBro is essential reading."

    – Chaz Kangas, Go 95.3 FM / Village Voice

"*Bernard writes with bravery, humor, and grit about his fight with testicular cancer. At a time when we're looking for more healthy definitions of masculinity, take note: It takes a real man to write this honestly about his junk.*"
– Sarah Darer Littman, author

"*With ChemBro Adam Bernard has done more than document a journey, he's provided a public service for thousands of men who may be hesitant to investigate those nagging pains and mysterious aches we dismiss as insignificant. It's particularly timely in an era when the battle for healthcare dominates headlines and Americans are forced to prioritize between doctor's visits, rent, and eating. Using brave and accessible prose filled candor and heart, ChemBro pulls off the magic trick of making an enjoyable read out of a very difficult topic.*"
– Jerry L. Barrow, journalist

"*Who knew that a book about getting cancer and then beating it could be so much fun? Adam Bernard writes not only with a fine sense of humor but with a depth of feeling and understanding that will inspire all who read it. I find myself already looking forward to his next book.*"
– Chris Frantz, Talking Heads and Tom Tom Club

"*Adam Bernard fearlessly brings readers on a personal journey with 'ChemBro,' a clever, honest, and sincere tale about dealing with — and beating — testicular cancer. Despite carrying this heavy emotional burden (and, at times, a weakened immune system), he leaned on his martial arts and physical fitness activities to help occupy his mind space, as well as help to overcome his condition. Bernard's fearless warrior spirit jumps off the pages, and this book will undoubtedly help others warriors triumph in their own respective battles."*

— Bear Frazer, Chief Editor at ONE Championship

ChemBro: Embracing Beastmode to Beat Cancer
Copyright © 2020 Adam Bernard

Content Editor: Alexander Crawford
Copy Editors: Anita Gibson and Meagan Daquano
Cover Design: Kristi King-Morgan
Editor-in-Chief: Kristi King-Morgan
Formatting: Kristi King-Morgan
Assistant Editor: Maddry Drake

ISBN- 978-1-947381-36-0

Dreaming Big Publications
www.dreamingbigpublications.com

This book is dedicated to my family and friends, who have been the most amazing support system a guy could ask for.

INTRODUCTION

As you open this book (first off, thanks for that!), you might be asking yourself, "Who is this guy, and why is he so willing to be completely open about a topic as personal as cancer?"

To answer the first question, I'm Adam, nice to meet you! For the purposes of this book, I'm your bro. Not like your blood brother, but like a guy you fist bump at the gym, and who has your back whenever you need anything.

I'm also a longtime music, and entertainment, journalist, lifelong martial artist, and one of those crazy CrossFit folks. Don't worry, it's only like the fourth thing I mention when I first meet someone.

The answer to why I'm willing to be so open about such a personal subject – especially seeing as the type of cancer I was diagnosed with was testicular cancer – starts with multiple people in my life, especially those I worked out with all throughout chemo, telling me, "You should write a book!"

When enough people say something like that to you, you start to wonder if they're on to something ...

or simply on something. So I outlined my entire cancer journey — the initial pain, my first surgery, the entire chemo process, what I thought was my ultimate triumph, my second major medical hurdle, and my second triumph.

After looking it over, I thought, "Maybe my friends are right. Maybe I have something here."

Considering how active my friends were in supporting me, and helping me, while I was going through everything, I should've realized they'd know better than anyone!

I started writing, and it wasn't long until I realized why I needed to write this book.

This book isn't for me. This book is for anyone who is facing a hurdle in life (which is most everyone at some point).

I want to show people hurdles are meant to be jumped over.

This is where my definition of "embracing beastmode" comes in.

For me, beastmode means giving your all, whether it's in the gym, or in any other aspect of life. Beastmode is choosing not to give up when giving up is the easiest option. Beastmode is one more rep, one more mile, or when we're at our weakest, one more step. In short, beastmode is the push to accomplish more than you imagined you could.

With that in mind, I also want to show fellow cancer warriors that they don't have to give up their lives just because they've been told they have to go through chemo. You'll see that even with my testicular cancer diagnosis I not only maintained my lifestyle (with a few tweaks here and there), I managed to keep my sense of humor, finding quite a few laughs during the entire process.

Testicular cancer is a form of cancer that rarely gets talked about, and when it does it's done in hushed tones, like there's some sort of embarrassment factor because it has to do with our genitals, and many men associate their genitals with their manliness (weird how we never associate our chest and back hair with our manliness. If we could bring that back into fashion, I'd be the manliest man on earth!).

Had I not had a friend who'd gone through testicular cancer before I did, there would have been a host of things I didn't know. Having said that, an additional goal of this book is that I want to be that friend for anyone who needs it. I want to be your ChemBro.

So, this is my story. It's the story of a guy who simply wanted to treat cancer like an aggravation, and not allow it to define him, or prevent him from doing what he loves.

As a music journalist, I see anywhere from 100 to 150 artists live per year, and I wasn't about to let my diagnosis stop me from frequenting my favorite venues, or seeing some of my favorite people.

My communities at both my gym, and my dojo, are also an incredibly important part of my life. These are the people who continually push me to not only do my best, but to accomplish what I may have previously thought impossible.

I knew I had to continue my workouts in some way, shape, or form.

Before my diagnosis I had been invited to test for my fifth-degree black belt, which is considered mastery level, and was a goal a lifetime in the making. There was no way I was going to miss out on it.

I had some idea of what I was about to go through and felt that anything I could do that would resemble my normal routine was going to be a good thing. Life had to go on.

You'll see that through surgery, chemo, and a second surgery, I refused to miss a workout, and I refused to miss a deadline. I still went to concerts, and I still saw my friends.

Was it easy? I'd be lying if I said it was.

You'll read about times when I felt low, and even an instance or two when I felt slightly overwhelmed. Once again, that's where beastmode comes in, as ultimately, I came out the other side of chemo ready to accomplish a lifelong athletic goal. Little did I know immediately after that I'd be faced with another major medical hurdle (because apparently *just* getting through surgery and chemo wasn't enough, right?), but like I said – hurdles are meant to be jumped over, and just because someone tells you that you won't be able to do something, even if that person is a medical professional, it doesn't necessarily mean they're right.

Oh yeah, when it comes to medical professionals, I'm going to get into some specifics about doctors, and how to know if you've found a good one. Some doctors are great, while some don't seem to realize people are more than a diagnosis.

While the details in the following pages are my story, my hope is the heart of it can be your story, as well. If I can jump over my hurdles, you can jump over yours!

In the immortal words of Eric Cartman, "Follow your dreams. Beefcaaake!"

PART I
THE CANCER JOURNEY

CHAPTER 1:
ON BENDED KNEE

It was a Monday morning when it hit me. I was in the kitchen, making breakfast, which for me consists of heating up oatmeal in the microwave. I don't want to give anyone the false impression that I'm working multiple omelet stations immediately after waking up ... or ever, for that matter.

I felt a pain on the left side of my groin.

As a lifelong martial artist, and someone who's been weightlifting, and enjoying CrossFit, for a number of years, groin strains were nothing new to me. An over-aggressive roundhouse kick, a squat where I went a bit overboard, I'm not saying this was the norm, but it's certainly something I'd experienced in the past.

So I thought this was just another strain, although it did seem odd that it happened while I was just standing there. It also seemed odd that it was, far and away, the harshest groin strain I'd ever experienced.

In an act I can only describe as the most painful of proposals, I essentially dropped down to one knee.

That was new.

Being fairly bullheaded, I attempted to massage my inner thigh for a bit, then proceeded to eat breakfast, and hit the gym. My feeling was, since I was planning on working out my upper body, the pain wouldn't be a big deal, and I could get that muscle back to normal with a bit of light cardio.

The plan worked, for a little while, as the pain went back down to being what I deemed normal for a strained groin.

Everything was fine until I showered that night. As I was soaping up, I realized that while my right testicle felt perfectly normal, my left one was rock hard, and hanging a bit low. It was almost as if there was a decent sized stone in there.

I decided right then that if the pain, and this issue, was still there at the end of the week, I would call a doctor.

Yes, that's right, while a sane person would have called a doctor right away, or at least the next morning, my ass decided to wait it out. To be fair to me, this technique had worked almost every time for the entirety of my life.

Now, for me, calling a doctor is a very big deal. At age 38, I didn't go to regular visits with a physician of any kind, only having seen a doctor a few times since my 30th birthday, and those times were for specific ailments. This meant I didn't actually have a doctor to go see.

When Friday came around, I was still in pain, so I went to my health care provider's website to see which doctors in the area were covered under my plan and accepting new patients.

After doing a little research on a few doctors, I called one, and told the person who picked up that I was a new patient, and I had a severe groin strain I needed looked at. A few questions about my ailment later, she asked me to wait on the line while she found a nurse for me to speak with. When she returned and put the nurse on, I once again explained my situation. The nurse told me I didn't need a general practitioner; I needed a urologist.

At the time, my entire knowledge of urologists came from the times I used to hear my grandfather talk about making appointments with his. I assumed they were only for older people. At 38, how could I possibly need one?

I trusted the nurse, though, asked for a recommendation, and went back to doing more research.

The best I could do as far as an appointment was two weeks away, so I took that time slot, and popped a few store brand Advil per day until then. To illustrate how rarely I use any kind of drugs, the bottle I was popping those pills from had technically expired a few years prior. Hey, they still worked, and my feeling was the best-case scenario would be this pain would go away in two weeks' time, at which point I could cancel the appointment, and get on with my life.

Since you're reading this book, you already know I didn't get to cancel that appointment. In fact, by the time it came around on January 27th I was borderline thrilled to be there, as not only had the pain not gotten any better, the swelling had reached a point to where it was uncomfortable to wear jeans, or sit in what would normally be a comfortable position.

I knew something was wrong. I knew what the absolute worst case scenario could be, but I'd read a bunch of articles about groin pain – my Google search auto-fills were a bit nutty for a while, if you'll pardon the pun – and I was hoping it was one of the litany of other possibilities I read about. In reality, I was hoping I could walk into my appointment, hear the doctor say something along the lines of, "Oh, that's just XYZ. Just do these three things, take two of these pills a day, and see me in a few weeks."

My ideal scenario was blown out of the water in a three-hour timespan.

CHAPTER 2:
A THREE HOUR TOUR

You know how I mentioned that I'd only known about urologists through hearing my grandfather talk about making appointments with his? Well, when I walked into the waiting area at Dr. Kingsly's office I lowered the average age in there by about a million. Everyone – with the exception of the staff – was ancient.

After filling out some paperwork I flipped through an issue of *Sports Illustrated* while Ed Sheeran's "Shape Of You" played over a radio situated in a corner. Ironically, or perhaps poetically, there was an article about Erin Andrews where she discussed her cancer diagnosis.

I don't remember how much time went by, but once my name was called it didn't take Dr. Kingsly long to assess the situation. After a few questions he told me to drop my pants – Sadly, I've never had a date where that's happened after such little time – and after a quick once over he scheduled a blood test, and an ultrasound for right then and there. He even mentioned to the person making the in-building calls to make sure they could happen as soon as humanly possible.

That probably should have been a tip off that something was really, really bad, but a small part of me just figured this was a doctor doing his due diligence before giving his diagnosis.

The blood test happened almost immediately, and I then went downstairs to the area where they conducted the ultrasounds. This was yet another waiting area where I stuck out like a sore thumb. This time everyone else was a woman, and no matter how much I desperately wanted to have a conversation to break up the silence, everyone else was inside their own head, as well.

I waited, and waited, and waited for my name to be called. It seemed like everyone was being taken before me, even folks who arrived long after I had. I knew this was because they had actual appointments, and I was just being fit into the schedule, but for some reason I also viewed this as a good sign, like maybe it isn't *that* bad if they can be so chill about me being here.

A gray-haired ultrasound tech stuck her head into the waiting area and announced a woman's name. That woman got up, gathered her things, and went in. A different gray-haired ultrasound tech stuck her head into the waiting area and announced another woman's name. That woman got up, gathered her things, and went in. I thought, well, I know the area of the body where my ultrasound is going to happen, so it's a good thing I'll be dealing with a grandma – no chance of accidental arousal.

Right as I was having this thought a young, adorable, ultrasound tech with glasses stuck her head into the waiting area. In my mind I was thinking "Oh God, don't say my name. Don't say my name! Anyone but me!"

In a slightly perky manner she announced, "Adam, I'm ready for you."

DAMMIT!

OK, it's cool, just think about sports. Think about sports. This can't last all that long, right? It's just a quick ultrasound. It's not like my testicle is gigantic. I'll just remember every New York Mets lineup I can think of, and it will be over before I know it.

The tech led me to a room, apologized for the cold temperature – cue George Costanza shouting, "I was in the pool!" – and told me to take off my pants and underwear. Again, on dates this never happens this quickly!

I was given some towels to "cover up" with on the table, but once she came back in I knew there'd be significant handling of an area that could very easily lead to me giving an accidental show of emotion.

Baseball, Adam. Think of baseball. Think of baseball, and stare at the ceiling tiles. There is nothing sexy about ceiling tiles. Well, unless one of those women from HGTV are installing them. Dammit Adam, focus! Focus on the boring tiles!

The tech came back in, and went to work with the ultrasound machine, and a significant amount of lubricant that was actually quite warm.

She asked me a few questions, and I fairly successfully struck up a conversation with her about anything other than where her hands were, and what she was taking pictures of. The ultrasound process, however, was taking much longer than expected, at least it was taking longer than *I* expected. It felt like I had been staring at those ceiling tiles for a solid 20 minutes.

At one point she apologized for things taking so long, noting she likes to take a lot of pictures. Hey, I can respect thoroughness, although I did let her know I wouldn't be using any of these shots for my online dating profile.

After managing to make it through the ultrasound process without ... showing emotion ... I was given some towels to clean up with, and told to go back up to Dr. Kingsly's waiting area.

In total, with the original appointment, the blood test, and the ultrasound, I'd spent three hours in that particular medical building when my name was called again, and I sat down in Dr. Kingsly's office for the second time.

He told me the tests confirmed what he'd originally thought, and that I had testicular cancer.

It almost felt as though "cancer" was slipped in there, like it was just another word. My mind completely glazed over after he said this. I could not concentrate on what was said afterward – other than the slightly mind-easing 99% recovery rate – until he remarked that I needed to have surgery *immediately* to remove the tumor. That jolted my brain back to full attention.

Apparently, the pain I had originally felt, the pain that had forced me to take a knee, was the tumor tearing, and bleeding. I'd be lying if I didn't say I felt like a little bit of a tough guy, in retrospect, for having a tumor tear, and bleed, and then be like, "Walk it off, champ. Time for the gym."

Speaking of the gym, one of my first questions was, "When will I be able to get back to working out?" He told me most people take a month to recover. When I pressed and asked how long it takes an athlete to recover, he kind of begrudgingly told me two weeks is the earliest people come back. He added that he thought I'd be fine to walk around NYC within that timeframe, as well.

I'm pretty sure he sensed I was going to do both of those things no matter what he said.

My goal of getting back into the gym wasn't just for vanity's sake – earlier in the month I had been invited to test for my fifth degree black belt in Kempo, a test that would take place in June, and as someone who's spent his entire life studying the martial arts, I didn't want anything to derail me from training for this.

I'd also become heavily involved in CrossFit over the past handful of years, which was an extension of my being a gym rat. I found my CrossFit workouts were helping me greatly in the martial arts in terms of both strength and flexibility, so I guess you could say it was love at first lift … or love at first kick … whichever you choose, it was love.

Fitness, and being healthy, is something I've been passionate about for my entire adult life. It gives me a feeling of accomplishment, makes me feel good, there's a great sense of community involved, and yeah, I like what I see in the mirror. All of this made the cancer diagnosis even more confusing to me.

When I asked what caused my testicular cancer, noting I eat right, exercise, and I'm in great shape, Dr. Kingsly had a two-word answer – "Bad luck."

So, what had started as a doctor's appointment to see what was wrong, turned into me being seated next to a woman in Dr. Kingsly's office who was scheduling me to get my left testicle removed in five days. Dr. Kingsly was pretty adamant about getting this done immediately, although first he wanted a CAT Scan, so as I sat there – and I will admit tears were welling up in my eyes – I was having a CAT Scan, and surgery, scheduled for the following week.

That'll mess up just about anyone's plans.

CHAPTER 3: THE TELL-ALL

I texted my parents from the doctor's office to ask if they were home. When they replied yes, I told them I was going to swing by. I added that they needed to be braced for bad news, because I wouldn't be coming over if it was good.

I wasn't about to tell them their only child has cancer via text, or over the phone.

As I made the drive to their place, which was only about 15 minutes away, I tried to formulate what I was going to say. In all honesty, actually saying the phrase "I have cancer" was so much harder to get out than the diagnosis was to hear. It was an admittance of the diagnosis. It was an admittance of something being seriously wrong. It was an admittance of not being indestructible, which, yes, I kind of viewed myself as.

I pulled into their driveway with a heavy heart, and a metaphorical lump in my throat – in addition to the very real one in my left testicle.

Walking in, I sat them down and told them the news. It was an emotional situation, obviously. After explaining the details to them, my dad said it was "a real gut shot." I joked, replying, "I think it's more like a nut shot," and so began my traditional process of dealing with everything in life with humor. Humor, and a warrior spirit.

As I got back in my car I decided the next stop I had to make was my dojo. I'd been with my karate instructors – Jerry and Nancy Simon at Fred Villari's Studio Of Self Defense – since I was seven years old, and they definitely needed to hear this from me. Plus, being that the surgery was scheduled for the coming Wednesday, I wouldn't be in to teach the Thursday noon class, as I usually do.

The next stop after that was the house of my close friend Amy, who lives around the corner from the dojo (and would later stop by my place with a bottle of whiskey as a pick-me-up), I then hit up my CrossFit box to speak with my trainer, and good friend, Chris Skelton.

Everyone was equal parts shocked, and supportive.

Up next came the phone calls. I had a dozen or so folks I absolutely had to talk to about this, and each time I had to say, "I have cancer," the reality was further engrained in my brain. This is something I'm about to go through. This is something I have to handle, so let's kick cancer's ass. Let's make cancer tap out. Let's show cancer who's boss.

Late that night I wrote something to post on social media. I made the decision to share what I was about to go through with the world. I titled it *My Next Goal – Beat Cancer.*

The following are some excerpts from what I posted to Facebook, and linked to on Twitter, with some added thoughts on each selection.

Cookie Monster always taught us C is for cookie, and while that's a great rule, in general, as I sat there in the doctor's office today a completely different "C" word was mentioned, and my mind pretty much glazed over everything that was said afterward.

My doctor said he was 95% sure the tumor he found was cancer.

The word is horrible, scary, and whole bunch of other adjectives no one wants to think about.

The tumor is in my … ahem … man zone. The good news is that particular form of cancer has a 99% recovery rate.

How do you break it to your friends that you have cancer? I was trying to think of how it would feel to be on the receiving end of the note I was writing. Honestly, as I'd already discovered, there's no easy way to tell someone you have cancer, and there's no easy way to receive that kind of news, so I did my best to lead with positivity with the headline – I wanted to immediately let people know my mindset was a strong one – while also admitting early on in the note that yes, this is scary.

You also know I'm a rock when it comes to emotion, so what I'm about to say next might be a surprise to some of you … this is the rare instance where I will openly say I am willing to accept help. Sure, I think I can do everything on my own (only child syndrome), but f*ck it, you are all amazing, and every phone call, email, text, or visit is going to mean a ton to me.

Admitting I would need help was difficult for me. I'm very used to doing everything on my own, and as you'll soon see, in the early going I probably should have accepted more help than I did.

Even knowing I needed help, I was still, at times, too stubborn for my own good.

Please know my sense of humor hasn't changed … I could be angry, I could be morose, but neither of those emotions would help the situation.

I really wanted to emphasize to everyone that I had a strong mindset, and that I was pushing any negative emotions as far away from me as possible.

In the years before my diagnosis I'd worked hard to try to eliminate anger from my emotional repertoire, realizing that all it usually does is make things worse, and there's always a better way to handle a situation. With my diagnosis, I was about to go to war with cancer, and anger would only sap the energy I was going to need for the battle.

I will beat this, and hey, "Cancer Survivor" is gonna be a pretty cool addition to my resume, right?

I'm really good at finding a silver lining for most things in life. This was no exception. It was also yet another reminder to everyone that I viewed beating cancer as the only option.

Lemme tell ya, posting this was the best decision I could possibly make. The support that poured in was beautiful.

CHAPTER 4:
PARTYING > SELF-PITY

After I woke up to find a heck of a lot of people posting messages of support, I was reminded of something I've known for quite some time – I have incredible friends. What better way to celebrate this than by seeing some of them?

My friend Anna Rose had a show that night at Rockwood Music Hall in NYC, and knowing there would be plenty of other friendly faces in the crowd, and that I probably wouldn't be able to have a night out again for a little while, I hopped on the train and made my way into the city (if anyone's wondering, yes, it was uncomfortable to be seated on a train while dealing with an oversized, tumor-filled testicle, but I'd been living with the issue for weeks, so I'd kinda figured out ways to sit).

As I noted earlier, I'm not one for negative emotions, so while I could have wallowed in self-pity the day after my cancer diagnosis, I chose to party instead. Good friends, and good alcohol, were definitely in order, and there would be an abundance of both at the show.

Incidentally, this was one of those instances that make me think maybe Andrew W.K. has this whole "life" thing figured out.

Immediately upon entering the venue I saw a writer buddy, who put his arm around me, and as it sometimes goes with guys who are friends, words weren't really necessary.

Later on there were quite a few "You're gonna beat this," comments tossed my way (nobody likes saying cancer out loud. More often than not it was you're gonna beat "this" or "it"). All of which I appreciated, and Anna put on a great show, as always.

After her performance everyone made their way to the back bar (Rockwood's layout includes three stages – not counting Stage 0, which is just a bar – a back bar, and a green room that is curiously very red). Anna pulled me aside to talk. She'd known me long enough to not be surprised to see me out, still doing me the day after my diagnosis and sharing the note on social media. She gave me a hug and reaffirmed what others had been telling me – "You're gonna beat this!" I believe my reply was something along the lines of, "You know it."

This was a conversation I'd end up having with many people. Partly it was encouragement, and partly it was both parties attempting to handle the news. We're all human, and our humanity is one of the things that connects us all. This is something I would continue to see in the weeks and months ahead.

While in the city I soaked in as much as I could. One of the reasons I love covering shows in the city, and why I ride so many late-night Metro-North trains, is that there's a feeling, a vibe, that I catch there. I've lived within an hour of NYC for basically my entire life, so maybe I'm biased, but even as the city continues to change as the decades go by, I still feel good there.

I rode the train home happy that I made the decision to go to the show, and trying my best not to think about what I'd be going through over the next few days.

CHAPTER 5:
THERE ARE NO ACTUAL CATS INVOLVED IN A CAT SCAN

When I arrived at the radiology building for my CAT Scan I found another waiting room where I brought down the average significantly. In fact, with the exception of the staff, I think I was the youngest person there by about 40 years.

When an elderly lady needed help getting her walker fully open, I lent a hand, and held the door for her. She referred to me as "a fine young man." At 38, I felt like that was one of the few times I could possibly be referred to as young, short of hanging out at an old folks' home.

A few minutes later I'd actually be referred to as "young" again when the radiology tech called me in, and saw my age on the paperwork I'd filled out.

She was extremely nice, and let me know the stuff they'd be injecting me with would feel like a shot of whiskey. She wasn't lying.

I was told to follow the prompts on the screen, which featured a head that resembled Pac-Man telling me when to breathe, and when to hold my breath.

In the pre-CAT Scan "how-to" guide, when the voice explained which image represented holding your breath, it had "30 Seconds" next to it. I noted to the tech that I probably couldn't hold my breath for 30 seconds, and she said no one has to, and that she had no idea why they used that as an example.

So I laid back, again with my pants off – because if there's an attractive woman tech involved my pants must be on a chair somewhere – and I jumped through the hoop. OK, I didn't jump, I was on a table that moved me through the hoop, but I like making it sound more like a circus act.

I wouldn't get the results of the CAT Scan until after my surgery.

CHAPTER 6:
LIKE A SURGEON

On the morning of February 1st, as a nurse called my name, and opened a door for me, my nerves really became apparent. She instinctively asked, "How are you today?" I halfheartedly replied, "You have the chart in your hand. You know what's about to happen."

My father accompanied me – one, because he knew I wouldn't be able to drive myself back, and two, because he knew I wasn't going to be in the right mindset to actually hear everything the doctors would be telling me about the surgery and recovery. He was right on both counts.

I answered the same set of questions asked to me by three separate people. Part of me wondered if the repetitiveness of it all was part of the hospital's way of making surgery feel like a better option than having to repeat myself one more time.

Dr. Kingsly came in to let me know he was almost ready. I joked that he better make sure to take the correct testicle. He took a Sharpie out and marked an X on the left side of my hip.

Eventually the anesthesiologist came in, and introduced himself. I tried my best to play it cool, and make it seem like I was handling everything just fine. After I warned him that the only other time I'd had anesthesia I was later told I cursed up a storm the entire time, he started a slow drip.

My dad let him know that I was bullshitting about not being all that nervous, although he didn't use those exact words, and a few minutes later I was off to dreamland. By the time I woke up I was back in the room with one less testicle, and feeling more than a little woozy.

Somehow – and do not ask me how I managed to do this, because in retrospect it not only seems impossible, it also seems really f*cking stupid – I put my jeans back on, and after a few minutes someone came to wheel me out of the hospital.

CHAPTER 7:
WHEN "RUGGEDLY INDEPENDENT" MEETS "MASSIVELY STUPID"

My dad drove me home from the hospital, then picked up my mom, and the two of them came over to my place. They had offered to have me stay at their house, but I declined. I declined, in part, because I couldn't stand the thought of my parents – or, quite frankly, anyone – seeing me go through a struggle, and in part because I've always been incredibly independent.

At age 38 I'd lived alone since I was 22, and even lived in a single (dorm room for one) for three of my four years as an undergrad. I'm also an only child, and a freelance journalist who works from home. When you combine all those things you get someone who is a living definition of independent. You also get someone who, even when he knows he should accept help, doesn't want to admit to many of his surgery induced limitations.

Pro Tip – If people are willing to help you, accept it! This is a lesson I'd quickly learn, and, because I'm me, and I'm Captain Independent (a f*cking terrible superhero), it's a lesson I'd completely ignore.

While my parents were at my place they spoke with my neighbor, Mary, about my situation (my building is filled with amazing, supportive, folks), and Mary, who is in her 80s, and is completely awesome, proceeded to spend the coming days attempting to make sure I didn't do things like get my own mail (which I did), while also making some good comfort food, like homemade chicken soup (which was delicious).

It was during my parents' visit that I also needed to use the bathroom. This turned out to be an adventure I didn't see coming.

After the surgery the doctor put me in what I can only describe as a ridiculously tight version of an athletic supporter, just without the actual athletic supporter insert. It was a genital harness, if you will. So when I pulled down my underwear, which was an act that didn't feel great, by the way, I had yet another layer to get through. Hey, it was February in Connecticut, and layers are always a good look that time of year. High fashion!

I worked the harness off, but was completely unprepared for what I saw.

Having never had surgery before, I had no idea about swelling. Sure, I understood the concept, I'd just never seen it in action so up close, and in such a personal area on my body.

Warning – what I'm about to describe to you is graphic.

The area that housed my now singular testicle was f*cking gigantic … and purple. It was roughly the size of a softball, and with a similar consistency (the stitches were on my pelvic region, just below my left oblique, so at least those weren't down there).

I was shocked.

I was shocked, I was scared, and I was mad. The anger was from feeling like I wasn't properly warned about this in advance. The fact of the matter is, even if I had been warned, and for all I knew I had been, I stood no chance of remembering such a warning after I'd been knocked out.

Thankfully, a friend of mine, Jesal, had offered to talk to me about anything involving the surgery, as he had gone through it a number of years ago. I DMed him on Twitter that night telling him about my newfound issue. He assured me it was normal, and nothing to be worried about. When I spoke with my doctor the next day this was reiterated to me.

In addition to Jesal, I had a shoulder I could lean on at the gym who'd been through this surgery, and was extremely supportive, although I'm not sure he'd want his name in print, so hopefully he'll realize this is my way of shouting him out.

Getting back to my situation, when a scrotum is swelled to that kind of level, Mr. Happy becomes a scared turtle.

So here I am, needing to pee, but having very little to work with when it comes to aim. I managed to get into a fairly acrobatic position that allowed me to hit the intended target (praise the Lord for my ninja skills), but I wasn't thrilled at the prospect of having that be my go-to position for going to the bathroom for however long it was going to take for the swelling to go down.

Then came the prospect of having to go #2. There was no way I could fit that mess between my legs where it needed to be while I was sitting on the throne. The logistics were simply impossible. I was going to have to hold a container in front of me to catch the #1 while I did the #2.

Thankfully, in something I wouldn't usually consider good news, the stress of the surgery, and the pain relievers they gave me, caused me to, ahem, back up in the #2 department, so I didn't have to deal with that for a few days. (My folks would bring over one of those raised toilet seat contraptions, as we thought that might help, which it sort of did, but I actually ended up using it for something else entirely, which I'll get to later)

My parents, confident I could handle the evening on my own — or realizing I was going to do it on my own no matter how much sense they tried to talk into me — went home, and I attempted to find a comfortable position on the couch to watch a little TV. The doctor had given me a prescription for a powerful pain reliever, Oxycodone, that I was hoping to not have to use.

The next morning I woke up and found myself in the midst of another surgery induced challenge — actually getting out of bed.

For some reason I hadn't foreseen this issue. I guess I didn't realize a large waist-level gash was going to be more than a little inhibitive when it came to doing things like sitting up, and swinging my legs over the side of the bed. Lemme tell ya you *really* appreciate those little things when they're suddenly taken away from you.

Eight attempts later, and using a combination of gripping the sheets, brute force, ignoring pain, and gritting my teeth, I managed to get my body up and out of bed. It was at around this time I realized I was a total idiot for attempting to do all of this on my own, but, me being me, I wasn't about to admit this. I mean, I worked my way up, and out of bed. Sure, it was insanely difficult, but I did it, so in some weird way I felt like I proved something to myself.

CHAPTER 8:
THE FIRST FULL DAY

Starting my first full day of recovery, I decided I wasn't going to do any work the entire day. A total workaholic like myself doesn't come to a decision like that easily, especially since the affected area played no role in my ability to type – although I did find it sure as heck played a role in my ability to sit at my desk.

Unfortunately, this was also day one of not going to the gym.

I am not a sedentary person. I am also a person who thrives on the routine I've created for myself. Taking 60 to 90 minutes out of my routine, and out of being active, and replacing it with basically rest, and icing down my ridiculously swelled genitals, was difficult.

Here's what I learned over the course of my non-work, non-workout, day, most of which was spent watching TV.

1. The kids on *Dawson's Creek* were the most overdramatic high schoolers in history. Seriously, they spoke like everything was the end of the world, even something as unimportant as who they were going to take to a school dance.

2. David Spade has more shows in syndication that I thought humanly possible. Is there some sort of rule that every fifth sitcom pitched to networks has to include a role for him?

3. The lack of decent game shows is startling. I remembered from my youth that whenever I was sick at home there were hours of game shows to watch. Not so much so anymore. :(

My mind wandered. I started to do what a lot of guys do, and I'm sorry if I'm breaking this news to any ladies out there, but yes, we think up nicknames for our genitals. The nicknames had to be doubly creative for me now that I was three balls shy of a walk. Three of my favorites that I came up with were:

1. The Highlander ... because there can only be one!

2. The Wiffle Ball Set ... just a bat and a ball.

3. Almond Joy and Mounds ... because sometimes you feel like a nut, sometimes you don't. I actually wanted to find a way to get pajama pants where the left side was Mounds, and the right side was Almond Joy, to truly represent my situation.

After one of my least mobile days on record, I felt a pretty decent amount of pain and popped an Oxycodone before bed, wanting to be able to get at least a few hours of sleep.

I immediately realized why people get hooked on those pills.

Within minutes I had the feeling of being drunk, and high. Now, for me the effect may have been quicker than for most since I don't normally take any sort of over the counter drugs, let alone prescription drugs, but I had to imagine this is the kind of feeling addicts chased.

The next day, when I was in pain, I had one and the effect was nearly as great. It was at that point that I decided I wasn't going to use them anymore. I wasn't going to be chasing that high, popping multiple pills of that kind of strength per day.

I called my doctor to ask him what I considered to be a very important question – if I stop taking the pills, will I be able to drink alcohol again?

The answer was yes, and being that it's perfectly safe (OK, maybe not *perfectly* safe) to have alcohol and store brand ibuprofen, a nightly glass of whiskey seemed like a far more enjoyable, and less dangerous, way of medicating.

My father, who worked in the pharmaceutical industry for nearly 30 years, not only agreed with my decision, he and my mom came over to my place for the Super Bowl with a bottle of Jack Daniel's.

During my first week of recovery a number of friends also stopped by bearing gifts of whiskey, and conversation, both of which were much appreciated.

If you ever have a friend who's gone through surgery, and you have no idea what to get them, lemme tell ya, what they really need is someone to hang out with, because when you're unable to go anywhere, having people come to you makes all the difference in the world.

CHAPTER 9:
FINDING NORMAL

One day. That was all I could take of accepting the whole, "You need to get your rest" idea. My second day after surgery I wrote a column. I couldn't really sit at my desk, so I wrote it while in a laid-back position, with my feet kicked up, on the sofa. Hey, I was writing, I was accomplishing something, so I was happy.

A few days later the lack of being able to work out was driving me insane. I was happy I could walk up and down the long hallways of my building, and I could even, gingerly, make it down, and back up, the stairs, but a man that lives by the phrase "beastmode" can only be kept from said beastmode for so long.

I took a look at the raised toilet seat my folks had brought over. The handles on the side were perfectly positioned for tricep dips. I banged out a set of ten. Then I thought of all my martial arts training, specifically one of the tension-based forms we have, and I said to myself,

"I can't get to the gym to lift, but I can use this raised seat to do dips, and from a seated position I can do tension-based biceps, chest, and back exercises."

I started doing three rounds of each twice per day.

I then decided I would attempt to do a push up. Just getting into the push up position was a challenge, especially since I wanted to make sure I didn't rip my stitches. It would turn out I couldn't do one on the first day I tried, but I tried again the next day, and the next day, and on the third day of attempts, I made it happen. This is also when I felt it would be OK to attempt a sit up.

This was a bit trickier, as the stitches were at my waistline, but I figured I was getting out of bed pretty alright at this point, and doing sit ups would only help with that.

I managed to do a few before feeling like the stitched area might be in danger. Here was the good news, I could now add small sets of push-ups and sit ups to my tension-based workout routine, and when you do enough small sets they can add up to some pretty decent numbers.

I felt I was on the right track. A few days later, when I was able to add air squats into the mix, I started to feel whole again.

All of this, however, was done while being unable to stand up straight.

With the incision where it was, standing up straight was impossible immediately following the surgery, but each day I'd attempt to get my back a little more erect. When I started doing the at-home workouts it was the first time I started to really see an improvement there. I'm no expert in the field, but there is no way this was a coincidence. Working out makes you healthy, and working out, even just with these at-home exercises, was making me stand up straighter.

A handful of days later I was standing in my kitchen, hands on the counter, tired of being hunched over at the waist. I decided it was time to do what any manly man would do – I clenched my butt-cheeks and hoped for the best.

There was a very audible CRACK that was easily one of the loudest noises my body has ever made.

I stood there thinking, "Well, either I can stand up straight now, or I just paralyzed myself. As soon as I take my hands off the counter, I'm going to have my answer."

I took my hands off the counter and a wave of relief rushed over my entire body. I was completely upright!

I believe in miracles ... and butt-clenches!

Exactly two weeks to the day after my surgery I was back at CrossFit, working my way back to beastmode. My second day back I was doing 225 pound sled pulls. A few days later I returned to the dojo ... although I had to keep my kicks low, and to a minimum, until I was fully healed.

I was getting back to being me.

CHAPTER 10:
BAD CAT

Here's something you may not know about me – I love cats. This is why it was a bit upsetting when my CAT Scan results came back, and they weren't exactly what I was hoping for. Cats love me, dammit, why didn't this CAT Scan love me?!?!

The scan revealed there was a decent sized growth on my lung that needed to be checked out. Dr. Kingsly assumed the worst, thinking the cancer had metastasized and spread to my lung.

For clarification, this wouldn't be lung cancer, this would be testicular cancer that spread to the lung. This is an important distinction in regards to the treatment of the cancer. That said, I was, of course, hoping it was nothing.

The first step in finding out what I was dealing with involved seeing a pulmonologist, which is the super fancy word for lung doctor.

A friend highly recommended hers, Dr. Simkovitz, and her recommendation was co-signed by a friend's dad, who happens to be a retired doctor. Those kinds of recommendations make you feel good.

So I set up an appointment with Dr. Simkovitz, and after finding his office, a task that felt a bit like attempting to reveal a special entryway in the original *Legend of Zelda*, I was directed to sit in front of a machine that would measure my breath in what I still view as the most insane way imaginable to test someone's breathing.

The test consisted of a contraption being put over my mouth and nose, and having to breathe out for six seconds, multiple times. Six seconds doesn't sound like that long, but have you ever attempted to breathe out for that amount of time? It's a freakin' eternity.

Put me on a treadmill, make me run up and down the stairs, literally have me do anything but sit there and try to breathe out for six seconds.

The tests ended coming back fine, although that would be debated by other doctors who had their own agenda, and I was scheduled for a biopsy on my lung for the following week. Before that would happen, however – in fact, before I even went home – I was off to the next doctor's appointment, which was with an oncologist, who I was set to speak with in case the biopsy revealed the worst.

CHAPTER 11: DOCTOR DEBBIE DOWNER

It turns out not all recommendations are created equal, as when searching for an oncologist to speak with a few friends recommended someone I'll simply refer to as Dr. M.

Now, their experiences with this doctor were, I'm guessing, far different from mine, but mine was absolutely horrible, and an example of what happens when doctors treat patients as charts, and printouts, rather than people. Unfortunately, this wouldn't be the only time I'd have to deal with such a doctor (FYI, you'll immediately be able to tell the good doctors from the bad doctors, because for the good ones I actually use their names).

Again, as with all my meetings with doctors, my father cleared his schedule to accompany me. He referred to himself as my advocate. If any of you are pro wrestling fans you'll see some humor in this, as Paul Heyman refers to himself as the advocate of the beast incarnate, Brock Lesnar. I liked to imagine a scenario where my name was announced when I walked into a doctor's office the same way Heyman announces Brock's.

Once in Dr. M's office we sat down, and *eventually* he made his way into the room (we saw him walk by a few times and completely ignore us, which didn't give a great first impression). I handed him the CAT Scan results, and told him what my situation was, including my upcoming scheduled biopsy, and that I was wondering what the next course of action would be in both the best, and worst, case scenarios.

He said that if the growth was cancerous I'd have to go through chemo. I was obviously nervous about this, as the majority of what I knew about chemo was from television shows, and movies, that showed it to be something completely debilitating (the movie *American Splendor* immediately came to mind). Dr. M not only did nothing to ease my fears, he made them worse.

He told me he would recommend taking multiple months off work, saying that I would basically be an invalid, unable to move, or do anything for myself.

I let him know I'm a freelancer, and taking multiple months off isn't an option. He replied that *maybe* typing would be OK.

It was at this point that I noted his physique. Dr. M was a solid 50 pounds overweight, and bore quite the gut. I thought to myself, "I'll be damned if I let some guy who looks like this try to tell me what *my* body can handle."

Then he said something that completely eliminated any lingering thoughts of possibly using him as my doctor.

He told me *even if the growth isn't cancerous* he'd still recommend chemo.

WTF?!?! You mean to tell me that you want to put poison in my body just for the hell of it? F*ck you!

He then added that after the chemo he'd want to dissect my lymph nodes to see if there was anything hiding in there, and even if there wasn't, he'd still recommend *more chemo*.

Dissect was a word that really turned me off, and I think this illustrates the importance of language, and our choice of words. When I heard "dissect" I suddenly felt less like a patient, and more like the doctor was viewing me as his personal science experiment. Why? Because the last time I heard the word "dissect" was in a grade school biology class, and it involved dead frogs.

Had he chosen his words better he would have come off as a bit more caring, and a bit less mad scientist-y.

With his seemingly constant recommendation of "chemo no matter what," I was beginning to feel like this guy was nothing more than a chemo salesman. There's an old saying that if your only tool is a hammer, you start to see everything as a nail. That seemed to be the case with Dr. M, who then smiled when he went into great detail about the chemo unit they had in the back of the office. It was legitimately the only time I saw him smile, and the only time he seemed excited about anything.

We thanked him for his time — although my father and I agreed afterward that there was no way I'd be using that guy, no matter what — and left.

My frustration at this point was very real, and the 225 pound sled pulls the next morning felt great.

CHAPTER 12: BIOPSY BLUES

I received a call the evening before my biopsy with the typical information of needing to fast starting at midnight, what time I should show up at the hospital, a reminder that I'd need someone to drive me home, yadda yadda yadda. An added bit of information that would turn out to severely swing the process was that the doctor that Dr. Simkovitz has set all this up with had a death in the family, and would be at a funeral, so I would be having my biopsy done by a replacement.

I met the replacement doc, Dr. H, and his team of assistants, two of whom were especially memorable, one because he was kind, and covered in colorful tattoos, and another because he seemed to understand each patient is actually a person, and treated me as such.

For the biopsy I was going to be put half-under. Basically, I'd be awake, and able to respond to commands, but I wouldn't be able to feel what was going on. What was going on was a giant needle was being inserted into my back, aimed at the growth on my lung.

I was informed beforehand that very rarely does the needle poke a hole in the lung, and in those cases the lung heals on its own. In only the most extreme cases does a puncture result in a lung collapsing. All I could think was, if you screw this up so badly my lung collapses, we're gonna be on the news, cuz you're gonna get your head handed to you by a guy with only one functioning lung!

I was also advised not to do heavy cardio for a few days. So if I had to give the doc an ass whoppin' I'd have to do it without raising my heart rate.

The actual procedure felt very strange. I'm not entirely sure what went on, as I couldn't exactly turn around to look at my back, but it felt like someone was building a pentagon shaped building with LEGOs on my back. I never felt a needle go in, just a lot of tapping.

Afterwards I was taken back to the little area full of empty beds to await the results. This is where things got hairy ... and I don't just mean my back!

They wanted to take an X-ray to make sure they hadn't punctured my lung. You know, that thing they said only rarely happens. Guess what, it happened. That shouldn't really be a major issue, though, right? They said the lung heals itself. I'll just take it easy.

Nope. They wanted me to hang around and take another X-ray in a few hours. OK, I'll hang around, just lemme get some food, or a protein bar. I mean, I hadn't eaten since the night before, and we were in the afternoon now. As a workout freak, that means I've missed four meals!

Nope. They said I can't eat or drink anything, except a small cup of water, because if the lung collapses they'll have to insert a breathing tube, and if I ate they'd have to do that without anesthesia!

At this point I was getting skeptical of the doctor, because this sounded less like care, and more like a scare tactic.

Still, I waited, they took another X-ray, and they once again said they wanted me to wait a few hours and to take another. Again, I said I'd like some food of some kind. At this point I'd missed five meals, and it had been well over 14 hours since I'd last eaten.

Nope. No food for me! Just another tiny glass of water. To top things off, I was yelled at by an aide when I got up from my bed to stand up and stretch my legs. How dare I move! I could collapse!

The BS was strong with this one. She even called the doctor and all of his people back in to "talk" with me and my father. This was no ordinary talk, however, as the team surrounded my bed on all sides, and attempted to scare me into doing everything they said. It was the closest I've felt to being bullied since grade school, and I was pretty sure I'd get in a lot of trouble if I swung on any of these folks (yes, I have bullying stories, but those are for another time).

I attempted to reason with them, but they weren't hearing it. Eventually they agreed to get the next X-ray done as quickly as possible.

There was still a small hole. This is when the sh*t hit the fan, because they once again requested I go two more hours without food.

This time I said nope, and my father said nope.

The thing you need to know about my dad, in addition to being a lawyer, he's also an operatically trained baritone, and he doesn't take kindly to attempts at intimidation.

I heard the entirety of a heated discussion he had with the doctor, which involved asking about leaving against doctor's orders. The doctor said something along the lines of, "You can do that, you just have to know your son could die!"

That was definitely the last straw. I was actually surprised my dad didn't knock him out.

I checked out against doctor's orders, and set up a time to come back the next morning to get another X-ray (which would reveal the hole was gone).

To say I enjoyed my first meal in 16 hours would be an understatement.

Unfortunately, my joy would be trampled on when I learned the results of the biopsy – the growth on my lung was more cancer.

Thus I began a quest to find out as much as possible about all my options before making a decision on treatment. Of course, since I'm me, while doing research, and setting up appointments with doctors, I still found time to fit in some fun.

CHAPTER 13:
BACK IN THE CITY

On March 4th I finally felt like the swelling down under had gone down enough for me to get into a pair of jeans for an entire night, and take the train into the city.

I had not one, but two events I wanted to go to – my friend Super King Armor's show at Leftfield, and my friends Chaser Eight's show at Pianos. The scheduling gods were clearly smiling on me, as Super King Armor's show was early, while Chaser Eight's show was later, and the venues were only a block away from each other.

This turned out to be a truly epic night, as it started with me seeing over a dozen friends, one dating back to college, at Super King Armor's event. Everyone was stoked to see me out and about, and looking well, and I even corralled a few folks who attended that show to head with me to the next one.

Oh, did I mention drinks were purchased. *Numerous* drinks were purchased.

We made our way to Pianos, where everyone I brought became fans of Chaser Eight as soon as they heard them (their hard rock cover of Adele's "Hello" is pretty amazing). This meant a lot to me, as Chaser Eight are a Connecticut-based band, and while I write a lot about NYC artists, I'm also pretty passionate about my favorite acts from the state in which I reside.

Oh, and more drinks were purchased. *A lot* more drinks were purchased.

I'm not going to say how many drinks I had, because, quite frankly, I don't remember, I just remember the fear I felt when a friend handed me another whiskey and I had no idea how I was going to manage to drink it. Let's just say everyone in the room became *really* attractive.

I was planning on making my way to the train station to take a late train home when the band let me know they had room in their van for one more, so I hitched a ride home with them. It was a ride that included a random stop at a late-night chicken spot in The Bronx, not to order chicken, but to make a bathroom run. I guess someone must have had a drink while we were there, or the place wouldn't have let us use their restrooms en masse.

All in all, it was an incredibly memorable night filled with friendship, music, and alcohol.

CHAPTER 14:
THAT'S NOT A KNIFE

If you've ever channel surfed up into the channels that are triple digits, and air reruns of old sitcoms, you've probably seen a commercial for a medical procedure called CyberKnife. The ad features a minister, I actually think his official title is apostle, talking about how when he was diagnosed he put his faith in God, and the CyberKnife doctors at whatever hospital they were advertising.

After the scare of being told I wouldn't be able to move if I were to do chemo, I was interested in knowing more about CyberKnife, and seeing if I could find a doctor in my area who specialized in the procedure.

While starting that research, I also scheduled an appointment with Memorial Sloan Kettering in NYC, as they're universally regarded as one of the top cancer hospitals in the country. Unfortunately, they weren't in-network for my insurance, so I later received a bill that I had to pay in full.

Before my appointment in the city, I found a CyberKnife doctor in Stamford, Dr. Dowling. I was pretty excited at the prospect of not having to go through chemo, and simply having this tumor zapped out of me over the course of a few treatments.

Unfortunately, my excitement was short lived, as when I met with Dr. Dowling he informed me that CyberKnife was not an option in my particular case. Apparently testicular cancer is so responsive to chemo that it wouldn't make sense to get rid of the tumor any other way. He also noted that since it had metastasized there was a chance it could be elsewhere in the bloodstream, and chemo would get rid of that, while CyberKnife wouldn't.

Dr. Dowling didn't only deliver bad news, however. When I told him about my previous encounter with an oncologist, and why I was trying to avoid chemo, he told me that I had been completely oversold on the effects of chemo, and that he knew an oncologist in my town that would be a perfect fit for me, and my lifestyle.

Not only did he give me the oncologist's name and number, he called him up to tell him about me, and my situation.

While I was dejected that it seemed as though I was going to have to go through chemo, I was slightly heartened by the idea that chemo wasn't a life killer.

The next day I hit the city to go to Memorial Sloan Kettering to meet with a doctor there, and ask a plethora of questions.

CHAPTER 15: EXPENSIVE INFO

As I noted in the previous chapter, Memorial Sloan Kettering was out of network for me, meaning my insurance wasn't going to cover a penny of the cost of the appointment. That said, I felt with their reputation, and having a meeting with a doctor there who had worked with athletes, it was the right place to gather information about the chemo process, and how I could handle it.

The total bill for the half hour, or so, I was there was significant, but the information was valuable, and the visit put my mind at ease about a lot of things.

I rode the train into the city in the morning feeling the strange sensation of knowing I'd be seeing the city in the daylight. As a music journalist, I'm almost exclusively there at night, covering concerts, so this whole sunshine thing was a bit of a revelation. I joked with my dad that I may not know my way around with the sun out.

I met with Dr. Funt at Memorial Sloan Kettering. He was young, and asked me a lot of questions, which is something I felt good about. The first oncologist I met with, the one that felt like a chemo salesman, didn't ask me anything. This guy, on the other hand, not only wanted to get the full story, he wanted to know about my daily life.

I can't stress enough how huge this is.

When a doctor wants to know about a patient's daily life it shows they're actually going to think about their medical recommendations, rather than simply seeing a diagnosis and say, "Well, you have X, so you have to do Y."

After Dr. Funt heard my full story I started asking him questions, specifically, workout questions. I'd obviously heard that chemo can be debilitating to the human body, and I was interested in knowing how other athletes who'd trained through their treatments held up, and what they did to stay in the gym.

He informed me that I could, and should, continue working out, as working out actually helps prevent fatigue. I think it has to do with endorphins, or something (hey, he's the doctor, I'm just the guy who listened to him).

This had me doubly pleased, because not only had I been given the green light to continue working out, I'd been told working out would stave off one of chemo's worst side effects! Take that, first oncologist!

Dr. Funt advised me not to lift super heavy, as chemo has some major effects on the blood, and he had an experience with a power lifter who popped a blood vessel in his eye while lifting during chemo.

I jotted down that I would be backing off the weight during my treatments.

After all was said and done I left Dr. Funt's office with a renewed spirit that I could face this head on, and quite literally kick cancer's ass.

CHAPTER 16:
THE DUDA ABIDES

A handful of days after my spirit enhancing visit to Memorial Sloan Kettering I had my appointment with Dr. Duda, who was highly recommended by Dr. Dowling, and had been told in advance by Dr. Dowling of my situation, and my previous meeting with the Debbie Downer oncologist.

I came in with high hopes, and within minutes I knew I had found the right doctor for me.

After a brief introduction, which involved me telling him that I knew I needed chemo, and I was currently looking for the right place to get it done, he did something I didn't expect, but that completely sold me on him – he asked me what I did for a living.

When I told him I'm a music journalist, he looked up from his computer, where he was typing notes, and said, "You can still go to concerts."

The fact that he wanted to know what I did for a living, and openly talk about how going through chemo would affect that, made a *huge* impression on me.

I didn't feel like just another set of charts and stats — this guy cared! (I later found out from my friend's father who is a retired doctor that he used to recommended Dr. Duda to all of his patients who needed an oncologist. That's some seriously high praise!)

We discussed working out, and the conversation I'd had at Memorial Sloan Kettering. He seconded everything I'd been told about hitting the gym, and how people who work out actually do better when it comes to dealing with the chemo-induced fatigue.

It would be impossible to overstate how important this conversation was.

Not to get all new age-y, but whenever you're going through something major, like cancer, it's imperative that you find a doctor who shares your energy. You have to find someone you vibe with, because you're going to be seeing a lot of each other. When you understand each other on this level, everything becomes a bit easier.

After our conversation I was given a quick tour of the facilities, including the chemo room, which featured seven large chairs, and a TV.

We set up a nine week chemo plan, which was three rounds of three weeks of BEP (bleomycin, etoposide, and cisplatin), with the first week of each round being five days of chemo, and the following two weeks just being one day of chemo each week.

He also gave me a blue business card that indicated I was a cancer patient. This was just in case I had to be rushed to the emergency room for any reason. The card would help me skip the line.

With chemo, your body goes through a lot, and doctors don't want cancer patients to be exposed to sick people. With an emergency room being a haven for germs, my "get out of the waiting room free" card was a necessity if, God forbid, anything were to happen to me during the chemo process. (Thankfully, the card was never needed, but I can't lie, if I'd been pulled over by a cop I totally would've "accidentally" included it with my license and registration. "Gee, how'd that get in there? Sorry, you didn't need to know that.")

I'd start treatments the following Monday, March 20th.

Before I started chemo, however, there was something else I had to do.

You see, having already had a testicle removed, going through chemo meant there'd be a slight − around 10-15% − chance of infertility after all was said and done, so if I ever wanted to have kids I was going to have to make a couple of deposits at a fertility clinic and get some of my best swimmers frozen for potential later use.

I found a clinic a few towns over, gave them a call, and made appointments to make deposits that Thursday and Saturday. I was told to avoid sex for a few days before the first deposit so as to make it as effective as possible.

CHAPTER 17:
SPANK IT & BANK IT

I remember driving to the fertility clinic in Norwalk, CT, and thinking this was going to be the first time I ever ... handled myself ... in a place where I didn't live.

I walked up the stairs, told the front desk I was there, and was immediately led by a female nurse (nurse? tech? I'm not sure of her official title) to a small room. There she handed me a cup, and some paperwork to fill out. I joked with her that I'd never had to fill out so much paperwork to do this.

After she gave me the run-down of everything I needed to fill in, and fill up, she showed me the large, comfortable looking chair, and small TV screen in the room. I did not see a DVD player of any kind, but she told me they had YouTube, and HBO GO, among other popular channels.

I thought, that's great and all, but I'm not here to marathon *Game of Thrones*, or watch my favorite cat videos. In fact, I plan on spending as little time in this room as humanly possible.

Can you imagine the guy who goes in there to make a deposit, and then suddenly decides, "Well, as long as I'm here, I might as well watch the last six episodes of *Ballers*."

After a certain amount of time I'd hope someone knocks on the door to make sure whoever is in there is still alive.

There was a brief pause after the nurse finished telling me all the medically relevant information. That's when I realized that while the TV is nice, I was probably going to need something more than that to get this job done.

I scanned the room and saw nothing. It was a spotlessly clean, unbelievably sterile, room with tile floors, a countertop with a sink, the aforementioned chair, and a few cabinets and drawers.

Finally, I asked, "Are there any ... aides ... to help me with this?"

She told me to investigate the cabinets and drawers, and to drop off my deposit at the window on the way out.

After she left I slowly opened the first cabinet. I'm not sure why I did it slowly. I wasn't imagining an avalanche of porn falling out on me, or a giant "gotcha!" sign.

What I also wasn't imagining was what I ended up seeing – medical supplies.

F*cking hot, right?

Since that wasn't going to turn me on, I opened the next cabinet in hopes of finding something involving a naked lady.

More medical supplies.

I was beginning to wonder if the rest of the world had a strange fetish I wasn't aware of. Is there a Reddit group out there for guys who are turned on by things they see in a doctor's office? Actually, don't answer that. I'm sure there is, and I'm sure it's filled with stories that would scare the living daylights out of me.

Finally, I opened a drawer, a drawer I would later notice had a small sticker on it with the word "Magazines."

Looking up at me was a fairly buff dude with an Old Spice guy grin on his face.

Did they put me in the gay porn room?!?!

I moved that magazine to the bottom of the stack and was greeted by a far more welcome face, and set of heavily tattooed breasts, as the majority of the rest of the stack was a collection of old *Fox* magazines {insert your own "What Does The Fox Say?" joke here}. For a brief moment, basically on instinct, I went to check the masthead to see who their editor was, and if they needed any music writers.

Yeah, sure Adam, the readership of *Fox* magazine totally cares about what you think of the latest Taylor Swift album.

I casually flipped through a few issues of *Fox*, carefully noting the use of shadow and light in the photography … and by "shadow and light" I mean naked women having sex.

Eventually I landed on a young lady named Breanne Benson, who was having a tryst with a man named Billy. Let's just say she was doing things with Billy's willy, and I left my deposit at the window as I exited the building.

If I ever have to use the specimens from that day to have a child I will have to find a way thank Breanne Benson for her contribution to my life. Maybe if the child is a girl, Breanne can be her middle name. If the child turns out to be an older butler from an '80s sitcom, we can use the name Benson.

I returned to the scene two days later to make another deposit. My oncologist advised this to get the most possible specimens. Better to be safe than sorry.

This time I had to wait for a bit, as it was a Saturday, and the place was packed. As I waited I noticed the song playing softly in the background. I kid you not, the song in question was The Wanted's "Glad You Came." I laughed to myself. Actually, I probably laughed out loud a bit. It was just too hilarious a coincidence. It was damned near poetry.

Eventually my name was called, and I was led to the same room I'd been in during my previous visit. Knowing the lay of the land this time around I side-stepped the viewing of the medical supplies and got right down to business.

After all was said and done, and I'd contacted some long-term storage facilities, I had a dozen vials of specimens frozen for whenever I may need them.

FYI – Even with the cancer patient discount, freezing your sperm isn't a cheap endeavor, so be prepared for some sticker shock if you ever have to do this.

UPDATE – I went back two years later to get tested, and it turns out I'm all good, so while I still thank Breanne Benson, it turns out I won't need to name a child after an '80s sitcom butler.

CHAPTER 18: BALD & BADASS

In-between appointments at the fertility clinic I had an appointment to get my head shaved.

My friends Jackie and Marisa own a salon in my town (shout out to H Salon), and I figured that knowing chemo was going to cause me to lose my hair, I was going to beat chemo to the punch.

Control is a huge thing when going through chemo, because chemo strips a person of so much of their control. With this one act, losing my hair would be *my* decision, and would be *my* doing. It was my way of saying, "F*ck you, chemo! You think you can take my hair? I'm not gonna leave ya any hair to take!"

When I told my old high school buddy, and longtime fantasy baseball compatriot, Anthony Gargano, about this he said he wanted to do it with me as a show of support.

I was floored by this. I also asked him while we were on the way if he'd informed his wife, Mandy, of this, or if it was going to come as a surprise when she arrived home later that day. (He'd told her in advance)

Anthony packed his two young kids into the car, and we made our way to my friends' salon.

As we unloaded the car in the salon's parking lot, and I took one stroller, and he took the other, it became apparent what we must have looked like to any passers by – the world's most ruggedly handsome gay couple.

Anthony, I'd just like to take a second to say I've known you for over 25 years, and I love ya, but you're a Yankees fan, and I'm a Mets fan, and I don't think that's the kind of mixed marriage we could raise kids in. I'm sure Mandy will be relieved to read this.

As we made our way in we were greeted with hugs, and, in my case, a few attempts at holding back tears.

Jackie shaved my head, and a gorgeous woman we nicknamed 92 – because when Anthony and I were talking about how we entered high school in '92 she noted that was the year she was born – shaved his.

It was an incredible show of support, and I'm extremely thankful he didn't let me do this alone.

Later that evening I debuted my newly shaven head at The Acoustic, which is my favorite local music venue, as PitchBlak Brass Band was playing, and I'd invited a few friends to the show.

Again, there were more hugs, more held back tears, and quite a few, "You're gonna kick cancer's ass" shows of support.

My friends wouldn't let me pay for a single drink, and the show was a blast.

Three days later I'd have my first chemo treatment.

CHAPTER 19:
ENTER CHEMBRO

A quick note before I start this chapter. During my recovery from surgery, and during the entire chemo process, my friends and family were so incredibly supportive of me I can't even fully put into words how it made me feel. If you were with me during this journey, and you're reading this now, please know that every single text, tweet, phone call, Facebook post, "like," letter, visit, and gift is etched in my mind, and will never be forgotten.

I have kept every single note that was written — some are on my desk, one even spent the entirety of my nine weeks of chemo on my fridge (because it was written by a friend's daughter) — and yes, I thought it was cool when three female friends sent me flowers. #BrosCanLikeFlowersToo

I was very public about everything I was going through, giving constant updates on social media, and anytime I was concerned if something I wrote qualified as an overshare, my friends proved to me that I was sharing the exact right amount.

The vast majority of the time I'm a rock for other people to lean on, but one thing I learned during all of this is that the people in your life want to be there for you, and having a great support system played an important role in my recovery.

If you're going through something major, like chemo, don't keep it to yourself. Don't feel you should suffer alone, or that you'd be a bother to your friends. Your friends will be the ones who will lift you up, root you on, and keep you going (or, in my case, as you'll later read, occasionally tell you to chill).

I entered my first day of chemo with a plan. Not knowing exactly how, or to what extent, the chemo was going to sap my energy I decided I was going to work out *before* my treatments. With my treatments starting at around 8:30am, this was a pretty big challenge for me.

Normally I get up around 6:45am, and being that I have a home office, I'm in my office, typing away, by around 7:15am. After a few hours of work I hit the gym, then come back and continue writing.

With this new plan I'd be hitting the gym at 5:30am. This required me to get up at 5am. Do you know what I realized that very first day? Whether you're going to bed at that hour, or waking up at that hour, 5am sucks. It's dark, it's cold, and you feel like you're in a horror movie when you're driving down the street and only see the occasional headlight.

Nevertheless, I made my way to my CrossFit box at 5:30am (FYI, this experiment lasted for a week, at which point I'd figured out how my body reacted to the chemo, and decided I could work out *after* my treatments). When I'd told my trainer, Chris, that I'd have to go through chemo, he created a special workout regimen for my nine weeks of treatments, focusing less on heavy weights, and more on mobility. I would still be lifting, but not as much, and certainly not at the weights I used to top out at.

On any other day I'd walk to CrossFit, as it's only around three quarters of a mile from my place, but on this March morning it was pitch black, freezing cold, and I didn't budget that kind of time to get there, so I drove.

I made it there exactly at 5:30am, and raced to the door. What I failed to recognize was the giant icy spot right next to the door.

WHAM!

I totally wiped out right in front of the gym, landing ass first on the concrete. Being a martial artist, I knew to slap out when falling, and that's exactly what I did with my left arm. My right arm, for some God unknown reason, was raised high, holding my water bottle upright, making me look like a crumpled Statue of Liberty attempting to retain some sort of regality.

As I was falling, two thoughts entered my mind

1. Don't hit the truck you're right next to. That would hurt you, and you'd probably dent the truck.

2. Thank God no one's here to see this.

Thankfully, I missed the truck, but as I was getting back up I heard a female voice shout, "Oh my God, are you alright?!?!"

D'oh, there goes wish #2.

I sheepishly rose from the ground, said, "I'll be fine, thanks," and went in to workout.

After working out, and showering, I packed up my laptop and made my way to my first chemo treatment. Why the laptop, you ask? Because I had another goal in addition to keeping up with a workout schedule that would see me in the gym, or dojo, six days per week. I also planned on not missing a single deadline for work, and this included writing three weekly columns, and booking and conducting artist/celebrity interviews.

The chemo unit had wifi, so I knew I could write, edit, and hand in everything while the drugs were being dripped into me from IV bags.

I know what some of you may be thinking – Adam, you're freakin' crazy! You're going through chemo. If anyone has an excuse to take it easy it's you.

While this may be true, I have a very Type A personality, and when you combine that with loving your job, and being a neurotic freelancer who lives in constant fear that his position will be taken by someone else if he so much as rests for a day, you get someone who doesn't take a lot of time off from work (side note: my editor told me I could take as much time off as I wanted, and that my columns would still be mine when I came back. I thanked her, but told her my plan).

Doing my job, and going to the gym, also provided something I knew was going to be necessary during the chemo process – it provided a sense of normalcy.

For a lot of people, chemo turns their entire world upside down. Heck, for essentially everyone it turns their entire world upside down. I knew about the hair loss, I knew that even though I was working out I would be fatigued more often than usual, I knew there could be nausea, and a myriad of other side effects that I'd face on a daily basis that would radically alter my life.

With all that in mind it was incredibly important to me to have some sort of normalcy in my life, and for me that was working out, and writing.

Essentially, my goal was to treat chemo not as a life altering situation, but as an aggravation.

I would now be working, for the most part, from a chemo unit, not my home office, but I'd still be working. My workouts would be a little different, but I'd still be working out. And God bless television, as my TV shows would still be on at their usual times.

Normalcy.

So on day one I had my blood drawn, had my vitals taken, and was hooked up to the machine that dispensed what was in the IVs.

There was a giant bag of fluids, an anti-nausea drug, and my three chemo drugs. On this day I had to have small baggies of the drugs first, to make sure I didn't have a reaction to any of them. This means I spent the better part of an entire day in that chair.

Thankfully, the nurses at the chemo unit were fantastic. I have to give a huge shout out to everyone there for creating such a great atmosphere. They are some of the most amazing people on the planet.

One day per week everything was moved to St. Vincent's Hospital in Bridgeport, CT. The mother of one of my neighbors happens to work there, and I have to say it was nice to see her smiling face on those days.

In the chemo unit the entire staff was upbeat, and fun, and they weren't about to let anyone wallow in self-pity.

I think they knew from the first few hours I was there that I was a character. Not a lotta folks respond to, "How do you feel today?" with, "My butt hurts, but that's just cuz I slipped on ice outside the gym this morning."

In addition to slipping on ice, I quickly realized I'd left my lunch at home. The head nurse, Nancy, took pity on me, giving me some chicken they had leftover from lunch.

It was sometime during this day that I took a picture of my bald self in the chemo unit, making a ridiculous face, while hooked up to the machine that was dispensing my drugs. I posted it to Facebook and Twitter with the note, "Chemo? More like chemBRO, amirite?" and the phrase "ChemBro" was born.

CHEMBRO

I used the hashtag #ChemBro with all my workout updates, and pics, and everyone loved it. I think it was partly due to the attitude I was showing – my spirit would not be broken, and I was still going to be the guy they all knew.

Somewhere around 3:30pm I finally exited the building, with an assurance that the next day I wouldn't be there nearly as long.

CHAPTER 20: LESSONS FROM CHEMO

If there's anything that writing for the internet has taught me, it's that everybody loves a list. Heck, that was even one of the sections we had at a site I used to write for. With that in mind, here are a few of the lessons I learned at chemo.

1. I hate needles. I mean I *really* hate needles.

When you're going through chemo you're given the option of being stuck with a needle every time, or getting a port. A port is a device they surgically put into you that they can simply plug the IV into each time you need a treatment. Unfortunately, the port comes with its own set of problems, one of the big ones being you're not supposed to bathe for the first few days it's in.

Could you imagine me, a workout freak, not bathing for three days? They'd have to find a closet to put me in for my treatments, because the smell would be so bad no one would want to be anywhere near me!

I also had no interest in a port because I felt like I'd constantly be thinking about it while working out. Sure, you're told you'll be fine, but most people don't put in the kind of effort I do, and I'm pretty sure pull ups and ports don't mix.

So I went with the needle every time, and every time I cursed. It wasn't just a random set of curse words, though, I always always *always* said "fuck," multiple times, through gritted teeth. It was a deep, aggressive "fuck" that the nurses ended up looking forward to each time I came in.

Usually I arrived before any other patients were there, but during the times there were other people in the room I would either apologize in advance, or one of the nurses would say, "Cover your ears, Adam's here!"

I think they placed bets on how many times I'd say "fuck" each time.

One time I said it so aggressively it caused a doctor in the hallway to stick her head in to see what was going on. The response was, "Don't worry, it's just Adam."

2. *The Price Is Right* is the ultimate connector of people.

While not everyone was into *Live! with Kelly* and whoever was her co-host on that particular day (Ryan Seacrest didn't take over until midway through my chemo), and Rachael Ray only connected with some of the patients with her segments on cooking, and choosing the correct bra size (I totally got in touch with my feminine side that day. Also, BOOBS!), everyone, and I mean *everyone* knew, and could get into, *The Price Is Right*.

On any random day during chemo there was an older Latin man, a middle aged African-American woman, a few grandmother aged women of various races, an Indian woman around my age, and a college aged girl whose mom accompanied her, sitting in the chairs alongside me receiving treatments, and when 11am came around, and the nurses changed the TV to *The Price Is Right*, we all came together to do what people do when they watch *The Price Is Right* — judge the contestants and insist we could have done a better job than they did!

All of us sitting there suddenly had an intimate knowledge of the price of macaroni and cheese in Southern California, and totally would have done better at the grocery game.

We all would have put the Plinko chip six inches to the left. *That* would have made it slide right into the $10,000 slot!

How on earth could that guy have thought those dirt bikes cost that much?

C'mon lady, you're gonna have to put more oomph into your spin if you want to hit $1 on the big wheel!

Everyone knows you pass on the showcase that doesn't have a car!

I swear, if we ever really want to have world peace, all we need to do is put all of the world leaders in a room together and get them to watch *The Price Is Right*. The bond will be instantaneous.

3. Drinking water will get you out of there quicker

Here's a little secret for any of you who might be going through chemo — bring a liter bottle of water, and down that sumbitch within the first 60-90 minutes you're there.

The drugs are only a small portion of what they give you while you're in chemo. The vast majority of what's being pumped into your system is fluids.

From my understanding – and please know I'm not a doctor, I was simply a patient – they want to make sure the drugs get in you, and do the job they're supposed to do, but they also want to make sure those drugs get *out* of you before they start affecting organs they could damage. How do you get the drugs out of you? By going to the bathroom ... *a lot*.

Most people don't drink enough water as is, and they certainly don't drink enough water to flush out these drugs, hence giant bags of fluids are part of the daily dosage.

My nurses saw me coming in with a liter bottle of water, and finishing it fairly quickly, and after a few days started letting me leave earlier and earlier, saying they knew they could trust me to drink plenty of water.

The thing they didn't want people drinking – coffee.

Coffee dehydrates you, and whenever they asked someone if they'd been hydrating, and the response was, "I've had my morning coffee," I knew an extra IV bag of fluids, and an extra hour in the chair, was in their future.

As an aside, they weren't thrilled with my daily sugar free energy drink, but with all the water I drank they decided I was going to be hitting the bathroom plenty of times during the day.

4. Once you meet, and talk with, other cancer patients, the self-pity parties non-patients throw for themselves become laughable

It's nearly impossible to log on to social media without seeing multiple friends and/or family members being ridiculously overdramatic over something completely trivial. From burning their toast, to missing the bus, to accidentally reading a spoiler about their favorite TV show, everyone is typing FML (f*ck my life) for just about everything.

Those types of posts are annoying when you're going through your everyday life, but when you're reading them while in a chemo unit, surrounded by other people who are going through exactly what you're going through, and in some cases going through even worse (I sat next to a few terminal patients), yet we're all smiling, joking, and attempting to make the best of life, other people's "FML" self-pity parties become laughable.

The Friday before Easter an older lady came in wearing bunny ears and a bunny tail. She also had some mixed nuts she was sharing on another day. When one of the nurses said, "She's giving away her nuts!" I replied, "I already gave away one of mine."

That was the vibe the majority of the time in our chemo unit.

With this in mind, my thought regarding all the woe-is-me types on social media was always, "If we can have this kind of spirit while hooked up to machines pumping us full of drugs that are essentially poison, hopefully you'll be able to find a way to get over your burned toast."

5. All the focus on the things that divide us is bullsh*t

This is less a revelation from chemo, and more a revelation from my social media postings about my diagnosis, surgery, and going through chemo. It's also less of a revelation, and more of a reaffirmation of a position I already held, but a lot of people don't seem to realize.

In this life we can, and do, find a plethora of ways to divide us from each other – race, nationality, culture, religion, political party, gender, sexuality, age, choice in music, heck, we'll judge someone based on the sneakers they wear!

I'm here to tell you all of that is bullsh*t.

How do I know this? Because whenever I posted about my situation on social media – White, Black, Latin, Asian, Indian, Middle Eastern, Christian, Jewish, Muslim, Republican, Democrat, Libertarian, Anarchist, male, female, gay, straight, bi, trans, old, young, hip-hop head, metal head, emo kid ... f*cking EVERYONE responded with love and support.

So yeah, we may all have different backgrounds, different concepts of God, different people we're attracted to, and even different ideas on how the world should be run, but we all have something in common – humanity – and it shows itself in a truly beautiful way when someone is going through their darkest hour.

That said, we shouldn't have to wait until someone is going through cancer treatments to come together based on this commonality. It's something we can do every day.

OK, I'll get off my soapbox now, and get back to the story.

CHAPTER 21: NIGHTS OUT DURING THE FIRST WEEK

Here's something that probably won't come as much of a surprise being that you've read this far in the book – I can push myself a bit too hard. I am well known for burning the candle at both ends, then finding a way to insert a wick in the middle of the candle so I can burn it from a third end.

My basic rule is I'll sleep when my body gives out.

This is not the healthiest way to live, but by God those nights when I pass out hard are freakin' fantastic! I wake up feeling like Superman, like I can pick up and throw a small sedan, or possibly even a four-door.

With this in mind, even though I had been getting up at 5am to work out every day, I still wanted to live as much of life as possible, so I had two nights out. OK, one wasn't really a night out, it was a dinner with a few friends who were in town from Florida that I used to work out with (shout out to the Kanes), and another workout buddy.

Dinner was good, as not only was it at a reasonable hour, the Kanes' daughter handed me a handwritten note of support. That's the note that I kept on my fridge for the entirety of my chemo treatments. There's something special about a child's handwriting reminding you to keep pushing forward (plus, I'm absolutely convinced both of the Kanes' kids are going to be superstars in life, and that autograph is going to be worth something someday!).

The second night out was a much later affair, as it was my annual fantasy baseball draft, which we get together for in-person, and always turns into a long, enjoyable night of friendship, random arguments, and alcohol. Funny how those last two go together a lot in life. Probably just a coincidence, right?

Anyways, I was unable to imbibe during this particular draft as alcohol and chemo don't mix. Actually, I was told one drink probably wouldn't hurt me, but in that type of atmosphere beers are kind of like Pringles – once you pop, you can't stop – so I opted, on that night, and during the entire chemo process, to not have any alcohol (in the end I was heartened by the ease at which I managed to accomplish this. Of course, I also wasn't going out at night, so the temptation decreased dramatically).

My lifelong friend Anthony started the league something like two decades ago – the same Anthony who shaved his head alongside me – and after we all arrived at the house where it was being held (thank you Derek and Lauren) he made a quick announcement before the draft started.

Everyone knew what I was going through, and in support he'd had a bunch of rubber bracelets made up in

Hofstra's colors, blue and gold (I did my undergrad work at Hofstra), with the words "Stay Strong and Have Faith" in black.

He handed one to everyone in the room. There were a lot of hugs, and I appreciated the heck out of everyone's support. I also appreciated the heck out of the fact that after everyone put on the wristbands there was a silent agreement to not treat me any differently. The jokes, the ribbing, the insults – they all still happened, and I wouldn't have had it any other way.

Heck, I even mentioned potentially changing my team name to Ball One, or One Ball Count.

Some folks may read some of the jokes I make at my own expense and feel I use humor as a defense mechanism. I don't see it that way. I crack jokes on a daily basis because I like making people laugh, so cracking jokes about my own situation was a way to both cope with what I was going through, and to help those around me cope with what I was going through. Additionally, it helped to create a sense of normalcy, and as I mentioned before, normalcy is what everyone who is going through chemo craves.

I have to admit, I faded during the draft. I'd been up since 5am, I'd worked out, I'd just finished my first full week of chemo treatments, by midway through the draft I was struggling to stay awake. This was well represented in the team I'd end up drafting (yes, league, I'm blaming my sh*tty season on cancer/chemo. Fight me! Also, there's a chance I may draft better when I'm drinking. Drafts and drafts? Hey, it could be a thing.).

I made it home at around 2am, having pulled a 21-hour day after a full week of chemo. I'm not sure how many people have done that before, but I'm glad I managed to make it happen, because it was a heck of a night of friendship and support ... and one really sh*tty fantasy baseball team (thanks for nothin' Adrian Gonzalez, Carlos Gonzalez, Steven Matz, and Jerad Eickhoff!).

As an aside – my buddy gave me the big bag of bracelets, saying he figured the people I work out with might want some. He was right. Damned near everyone I saw at the gym, and at my dojo wanted a wristband, as did some of my work colleagues who saw them in a video I posted on Facebook a few weeks later.

Those wristbands made it all over the country, and even overseas, as I know there's one in Amsterdam, and two in Buenos Aires. I also know a few will end up in Dubai.

It felt amazing to walk into the gym, and the dojo, and see people showing support in that way. I'd say it was like I had a whole team behind me, but it wasn't *like* that, it *was* that. It was Team Adam, and it meant the world to me.

CHAPTER 22: WHO WAS THAT MASKED MAN?

Here's something you may already know about chemo – the drugs totally mess with your white blood cell count.

White blood cells are those awesome little things inside us that fight infections. Before I started chemo my white blood cell count was ridiculously high. I'd only get a cold once every three or four years. My guess is leading a healthy lifestyle played a role in this.

After three weeks of chemo, my white blood cell count was in the toilet ... and then someone flushed the toilet.

My count wasn't just low, it was dangerously low. We *almost* stopped treatment, but my doctor was confident my white blood cells would eventually bounce back (surprise, he knew what he was talking about).

For this particular week, however, I had to take some extra precautions. First and foremost, I had to wear a mask everywhere I went in public for fear of everyday germs getting into my body, and my system not having enough white blood cells to fight anything off. Basically, in my white blood cell depleted state, a common cold could turn out to be deadly.

Here are a few of my thoughts regarding my week of wearing a bandana over my nose and mouth, and eventually a medical mask the nurses gave to me

1. I was absolutely convinced I was going to end up on the local news the first day I walked to CrossFit with a black Rocawear bandana over the lower half of my face (the bandana was a gift I received during a press conference many many years ago). With my black, sleeveless, Balor Club workout shirt (I think I mentioned I'm a big pro wrestling fan), along with the bandana, I definitely looked like I was up to no good.

I actually did an internet search the next day to see if I'd made any local news outlets, and was kind of a little disappointed there wasn't a story about a masked man walking the streets.

2. Whether it's a bandana, or a medical mask, covering your nose and mouth doesn't exactly do wonders for your cardio.

Love the taste of cloth? That's what you get a mouthful of every time you suck wind while working out with a mask on.

For as much as I appreciated the germ deflecting powers of the items covering my face, taking a deep breath became impossible, and I may have been the first person to curse Eli Whitney during a workout.

3. It's really easy to get the equipment you want at the gym when you're wearing a medical mask. For some

strange reason everyone is willing to part like the Red Sea and let you have anything you want.

I was tempted to write, "It's not me, it's you!" on one of my masks, because, in truth, that was the real issue. My breath was fine. It was everyone else's potentially germ-y breath that was the problem.

Related: I also had to wear full gloves – not workout gloves, but full gloves, fingers and all – to the gym, for fear of touching something someone with a cold had touched. My trainer recommended mechanic's gloves. I found a pair at Home Depot that worked well enough (and I later wore while cleaning out my storage unit. Look at me, finding new uses for things!).

4. You can very easily scare the sh*t out of people at the grocery store.

I live by myself, and a man's gotta eat, and there was no way I was going to risk going to a place like a grocery store, which is a place filled with people, without a medical mask, so I said looks be damned, I'm f*ckin' hungry!

I definitely received a few interesting looks, although I get the feeling more than a few folks understood my situation, because some of the glances seemed more knowing, and less perturbed.

There were still a few anxious faces, and I don't blame 'em. With the blue medical mask on I looked like a low budget version of Sub-Zero from *Mortal Kombat*, and if you saw Sub-Zero walking down the frozen food aisle you'd probably want to get the heck out of there too! (although, I guess technically any aisle can be a frozen food aisle for Sub-Zero)

I thought about creating a "who wore it better" picture, but thankfully my white blood cell count bounced back, just as the doctor predicted, and I was able to take the mask off after a week, and never have to use it again.

CHAPTER 23: HOUSE ARREST

Even after my face regained its freedom, I still had to deal with a number of low white blood cell count related restrictions, some imposed by my doctor and nurses, and one I imposed on myself in the name of my health.

First, I was told that due to my low white blood cell count, I should probably avoid dining out, and if I were to dine out, I would need to bring my own silverware, avoid all uncooked vegetables, and steer clear of any buffets.

The latter was something I actually already did. I'm not a germaphobe, but I don't like the idea of food that's been sitting out there, and people breathing all over it, and possibly coughing and sneezing near it. No thanks, I'll pay an extra couple bucks to make sure my food hasn't been near any of that.

Being that I had no interest in bringing my own silverware just to get a meal, I decided dining out was no longer going to be an option while on chemo. It was only going to be six more weeks, and the risk wasn't worth the reward.

It was also at this point that the chemo drugs were starting to affect my taste buds.

Apparently this is common among people going through chemo. Many describe it as food and drinks, suddenly having a metallic taste. I didn't experience it that way, but what I did experience was certain food textures becoming incredibly unappetizing, and in some cases, borderline revolting.

The turkey sandwich I used to have on a near daily basis was suddenly a no-go because just the thought of the texture of the turkey made me nauseous.

As a gym rat, I eat A LOT, and chemo patients sometimes lose weight because of these taste bud issues. When everything tastes awful, it doesn't really make you want to raid your fridge.

I viewed this as a challenge to make sure I still had the same amount of food intake per day, and somehow I made it happen. When one food became unappetizing, I had another waiting in the wings to take its place (mmm, wings).

FYI — after chemo was completed my taste buds slowly but surely returned to normal.

In addition to all the food, and dining out, restrictions, I was told it would be best if I avoided crowds. This meant, in my mind, I had to take a break from covering concerts.

Live music is one of my favorite things in the world. My homes away from home are music venues, and baseball stadiums. I can't imagine any better places on earth. One provides a great soundtrack while being surrounded by like-minded music fans, the other provides an enjoyable day in the sun with a beer in your hand.

Belinda Carlisle was right, "Heaven Is a Place on Earth," and those are my Heavens.

During a normal year I'll see between 100 and 150 acts live, and hit up a handful of baseball games (Let's Go Mets, and Let's Go Yard Goats!).

That said, I wasn't about to risk my health for something that would still be there in six weeks when I would be done with chemo, so I made the decision to politely decline all concert invites until then.

In actuality, in my mind the concerts weren't the big issue. I frequent smaller venues that specialize in indie music, so most of the shows I go to only have 50-200 people at them. What I was most concerned about was the fact that I use public transportation, and the idea of being on a train, or the subway, essentially trapped inside a giant metal tube for an unknown amount of time with a bunch of strangers and their germs, was something that didn't sound very appealing to me in my condition.

Basically, for the next six weeks I would be a ripped version of Howie Mandel.

I became jumpy at the sound of a sneeze, and even stopped shaking hands with people, opting for fist bumps instead.

The only places I went to were the gym (lots of open space, high ceilings, and for the most part, healthy people), the grocery store, and my parents' house for the occasional home cooked meal (thanks, guys!).

Incidentally, all of these restrictions made it extremely difficult to have any sort of a love life. Yes, I was still thinking about that. A single man is always going to be thinking about that, even when he's spending large chunks of his day having powerful drugs being pumped into his body.

I couldn't take a girl to dinner. I couldn't take a girl to a concert. I couldn't take a girl to a movie. Basically, Netflix and chill was my only option, and I wasn't even trying to "chill" like that. I legitimately couldn't be in public places, so all I could do was ask girls if they wanted to come over and watch a movie, or listen to some music, while I'd pray I'd be able to stay awake long enough to have a halfway decent conversation.

You can guess how well that went.

I had some buddies jokingly say, "C'mon man, play the cancer card," knowing damned well the "cancer card" is what was having me pass out before the sun set.

Hey, I thought, I'll always have that special room at the fertility clinic.

CHAPTER 24: HAIR TODAY, GONE TOMORROW

After three weeks of chemo, and seeing my hair start to grow back, I was beginning to wonder if I'd made a rash decision when it came to shaving my head before starting my treatments.

Eventually, somewhere around the fourth week, I started to notice it falling out, but it didn't happen in the way you see it happen in TV shows, and movies.

I need to preface with what I'm about to say by letting you know I wear glasses, and the prescription is pretty powerful. Basically, everyone is an unrecognizable blob when I take them off.

Of course, I take them off when I shower.

So one night I'm all done showering, and drying off, and I've put on some pajama pants and a t-shirt, when I put my glasses back on, and what do I see but a small amount of hair on the ground. Not enough to make me break out the Swiffer, but just enough to make me wonder, "Where did that come from?"

I looked in the mirror.

Everything seemed fine.

I thought, maybe I just somehow accidentally pushed whatever was on the floor into one place.

Over the next few days this phenomenon would happen again, and again, each time with the amount of hair getting more and more impressive, until one night I put my glasses on and it looked like a small woodland creature had exploded in my bathroom, sans guts and bones.

Again, I looked in the mirror, and again I saw no change.

What the f*ck was going on?!?!

Finally, and I don't know what inspired me to do this, I put my glasses on *before* getting dressed, and when I looked down, in addition to another mess of hair on the ground, I noticed I was almost completely bald ... down there.

Yup, Mr. Happy was sporting a bold new look, and I had to laugh because when I was told I'd lose my hair, I never imagined the hair loss would start *there*!

Over the next week, or so, more and more hair fell off my body. Hey, it was the first time I didn't have to worry about my back hair (sorry if I just ruined my image for any ladies out there who may have imagined my body was smoother than an old school Abercrombie model).

Interestingly, while my man zone, and back, went completely hairless, as did my head, my chest hair ended up looking like I'd simply shaved it down to look nice, and I never lost the hair on my arms, or legs. My eyebrows stuck around, as well.

Now, the hair that was left on my arms was cause for some hilarity, and pain, as the nurses always had to tape down where the IV went in, and every time I was done with a treatment they had to rip that tape off, hair and all. (It wasn't technically tape, it was something else, but the result was pretty much the same)

I thought, "Ya know, of all the places to *not* lose hair, I really would've been fine with my arms going bald for a bit."

My head going bald was an interesting story.

I first noticed it not in the mirror, but in the shower, as my hands would be covered in more and more hair each time I used shampoo (which was every night. Don't worry, I'm a clean dude). I never looked in the mirror and saw myself *going* bald, I just looked at myself one day and BOOM, I was bald. Totally, 100% bald.

This is when I started the hashtag #BaldAndBadass.

In addition to losing the hair on the top of my head, I noticed I suddenly wasn't having to shave nearly as much. In fact, it got to a point where only a few hairs were making their way up, and I only had to grab a razor once a week.

Some of my friends commented that they thought I looked great bald – most notably, quite a few women, and every single one of my friends who already sported the bald look, and who were happy to welcome me to their bald brotherhood, even if they weren't happy about the circumstances by which it happened.

I was glad they felt this way, because I didn't have any other options!

Personally, I felt like I looked like the origin story of a supervillain. You know, the part of a supervillain's story when he isn't bad, right before something horrible happens to him that turns him into a power hungry, hero hunting, evildoer.

Come to think of it, something horrible *was* happening to me ... hmm, maybe I *should* have been working on that laser to carve my name into the moon! (shout out to Chairface Chippendale)

In all honesty, I was going bald anyway, so I was treating this as a preview of what was to come. The good news is – and I will try to say this with as little ego as possible – I looked pretty good bald.

Currently I sport a close shaven look (after a touch up in April before it all started falling out, I didn't need a haircut again until September. That's some serious savings, yo! Although, not exactly savings that equate to the medical bills that came in, which is why I don't recommend chemo as a way to make yourself bald).

I did appreciate the lack of upkeep involved in having little, to no, hair, and the ease of not having to worry about my hair at all in the morning, or in the wind.

That said, for all the people who felt I should consider keeping the totally bald look, I thought about it, but for the time being it represents a difficult situation I went through, and it would serve as a constant reminder of it. Maybe in a few years, and a few more inches of hairline loss, I'll sport the look again. The good news is I'm no longer scared of balding, because when it really starts to go, I will, in the words of sports analyst Bomani Jones, bring it on home.

CHAPTER 25:
THE ONE TIME I SAID WOE IS ME

OK, I know I'm making myself out to sound like a total badass warrior for most of this book, and as a rule I avoid ever diving into "woe is me" territory in life, because I think it's bullsh*t, and it snowballs. I'm much more of a "suck it up" kinda guy, which I'm sure you've already noticed.

There was one time during the chemo process, however, that I momentarily pulled a "woe is me," but I only did it to the sky.

It was a week when I only needed one treatment, but for some reason the drugs weren't delivered on time to the offices, so even though I was there, and had been all hooked up, I had to wait until Tuesday to get it done. This meant I had to do it at St. Vincent's

Hospital, because that was the day everything was set up there.

That Tuesday I got in my car to go to St. V's, turned the key, and nothing happened.

I turned the key again, and again – nada.

For some reason, the universe had chosen that exact moment, the moment when I needed to get my chemo, to have my car's battery die.

I was livid, and I don't normally get livid.

I looked to the sky and said, "C'mon, aren't I already going through enough?!?!"

I started cursing up a storm. One of my neighbors walked by and wondered what was going on. I told him half the story, later telling him the full story when I had calmed down. He totally understood why I was so upset.

I quickly got on the phone and called the nurses letting them know I'd be later than usual. All the people in my building who'd offered to drive me places during chemo were, of course, gone, because this was a Tuesday morning, and people work.

The next call I made was to my dad. I believe I asked him if he had anything planned for the early afternoon. He asked why. I told him the situation, and he said he'd pick me up in 20 minutes.

We made it to the hospital, I got my drugs pumped into my veins, and later that afternoon, in a cold drizzle, AAA jumpstarted my car so I could drive to my mechanic, who had a new battery waiting for me.

There you have it, my one "woe is me" story from the entire chemo process, and it doesn't even involve cancer, it involves a car battery.

CHAPTER 26:
MAKING ADJUSTMENTS

When it came to my training, both martial arts, and CrossFit, I had to make some adjustments.

For the martial arts, the biggest adjustment, and the one I enjoyed having to deal with the least, was that I wasn't allowed to hit, or be hit.

There was a funny moment with my doctor when I asked him about this. I don't think he'd heard the question, "When can I hit people, and be hit by people, again?" all that often.

The concern was twofold – not only were my white blood cells so low I was open to being affected by just about any germ that might find its way to me, and human contact is the easiest way to transfer those germs, there was an issue with my blood, as well. I'm still not entirely sure what that issue was, but getting hit was totally out of the question.

Believe it or not, I missed being able to get hit (as did the people who normally enjoy hitting me). I missed it because blocking punches and kicks has been a part of my life for over 30 years, and not only was I no longer allowed to do that, I wasn't even allowed to hit bags!

Do you know how difficult it is to train for a fifth degree black belt test when the ability to strike, and be struck, is taken away from you? I basically had to fight the air while keeping up with my mastery of my forms, and techniques.

All that said, I was happy that I was still able to be in the dojo, train, and not miss a single session.

Over at my CrossFit box I had a different set of training issues. As I noted earlier, I'd been advised to not lift heavy while on chemo, so I had to scale down the weight a bit for all of my workouts.

Honestly, this isn't a huge deal. It can be viewed as a bit of a blow to the ego, because you're suddenly lifting less than you used to be, but when lifting heavy is literally life threatening, it puts it all in perspective.

The true bummer about this, in my case, was that my chemo treatments coincided with the CrossFit Open workouts. The CrossFit Open is when every CrossFit box does the same workouts and we all compare our times/scores. My goal for this particular year was to "Rx" every Open workout, Rx being short for "prescription," aka the weight we're all supposed to use, as opposed to "scaled," which is the same move, or a similar move, but at a lighter weight.

Chemo made competing in the Open an impossibility, but I gave myself a goal of being able to Rx the final Open workout.

Before I could get to that workout, however, I had to get through all the others, and one in particular was especially memorable for a number of reasons.

The workout seemed simple enough, as it was just thrusters (a movement where you do a front squat, and on the way up push the weight over your head), and double unders (jumping rope and having the rope go under twice per jump). These were both moves I had no problem with, buuuut I wasn't allowed to do it at the Rx weight because of the chemo.

I begrudgingly bumped my thruster weight down, and started the workout, which was timed. We had to finish in 40 minutes or less.

Normally, I'd have motored through this, especially with a lighter weight. My body, however, had other ideas.

I struggled. The thrusters, which I couldn't believe I was having trouble with at the lighter weight, became brutal.

Refusing to stop, I pushed through, and completed the workout with time leftover, but I was visibly upset about it taking so long. Noticing my despondency, my friend Owen, who is a trainer there, walked up to me and asked what was wrong. I told him I was pissed I took so long, especially at the lighter weight. He reminded me I still finished in under the allotted time, which many people don't accomplish, and I did it while going through chemo, which is insanely impressive.

I smiled, and allowed myself a feeling of accomplishment. I also realized this is how it's going to be for a little while, having to accept that I'm going to take a little longer than I usually do, but finishing is the goal, and I would always finish. Well, almost always ...

There was one workout where I nearly passed out.

This was on a Saturday, after my seventh week of chemo – my final full week of treatments – and the first thing we did in the workout, which was done in teams of three, was a sled push. I knew from the very first push that it wasn't going to be my best day.

I suffered through the main workout, and then a second workout – aka a "cash out" – was put on the board. It was meant to be done as a team of three, just like the main workout, but someone piped up that we should do it individually. That would be my body's breaking point, I just didn't realize it until I was halfway through. Even after realizing it, I still didn't want to quit. Owen had to stop me.

I had just completed a second round of burpee bar touches (when you do a burpee, but for the jumping part you reach up and touch the pull up bar) and was slumped over on a stack of plates (the weights kind, not a giant stack of fine china). I was seated on a lower stack, with my arms on higher stacks to each side. I'm pretty sure I blacked out at one point while doing the burpees, but I was determined to complete the workout.

This was when Owen walked up to me, put his hand on my shoulder, and said something along the lines of, "You're done for the day."

Now, bear in mind, this is a man who frequently wears a hoodie that says, "Suck it up, buttercup," so for him, of all people, to tell me to stop was a pretty clear indicator to me that it was obvious I was in dire straits (not the band, although that would be pretty cool).

I took his advice, and called it a day. Hey, I completed the first workout, and 2/3 of the second one. I still felt good about myself, although if I recall correctly I spent the rest of the day passed out on the couch.

CHAPTER 27: THE I WORD

What I'm about to say (err, write) may sound a little silly, but there was a word I had a really hard time wrapping my mind around that I heard quite a bit in regards to how I was handling my situation – Inspiring.

People were calling me inspiring on a daily basis. Folks at the gym, especially – seeing me push through workout after workout – used the word to describe me. They also told me that seeing me push through workouts in my condition made them realize there was no way they could ever quit on a workout. I definitely had a few folks say, "I look at you, and I'm like, if Adam's doing it, I have no excuse."

Getting back to the "I" word, whether it was someone at the gym, or someone calling me, or someone texting me, it kept coming up, and I kept accepting it, but secretly I was a bit uncomfortable with it. I finally brought it up to a few folks. The conversations almost always went the same way ...

Me: People keep calling me inspiring. It's nice, but I feel weird about it. I'm just trying to live my life.

Friend: Yeah, but most people who hear the word "cancer" don't do that. They let the cancer run their life. You're treating cancer as an afterthought.

When put into that perspective I finally understood what people were saying. That said, I still didn't walk around like, "Hey, look at me, I'm inspiring!" It was more just me doing me to the best of my ability, and if people drew strength from that, it made me happy.

An especially poignant moment came when a friend on Facebook posted that, despite having some fears, he went to a doctor to get his man zone checked out, and he did this because of my story, and reading my updates.

That was a big eye opener for me. Someone actually went and got checked out because of how public I was about my situation. Me being an open book – and now quite literally being an open book – was causing people to do something positive for themselves.

So I accepted it – I was inspiring ... but I was also spending a lot of time on the couch watching TV, so I was inspiring, but I was also all in for watching Smackdown in my pajamas.

CHAPTER 28:
A WORD ON MEDICAL MARIJUANA

I know this has been a controversial topic of late, and by "of late" I mean over the past quarter century, but lemme just stand up and say this – marijuana is fantastic medication when you're going through chemo. If you can find a doctor who is medical marijuana friendly, and you live in a state where medical marijuana is legal, get on the list, get your card, and get some weed.

Personally, I asked my chemo nurses about the prospect of medical marijuana, and they had some whispered words for me about how I could get on the list. Unfortunately, my address somehow ended up one letter off in the system, and because this is the government we're talking about, no matter who I called, it was never corrected.

That said, there are other ways to get marijuana.

A friend mine, who I will simply refer to as The Baker, was my hookup.

The Baker, knowing my situation, and having a special set of skills, would come over to my place with fresh batches of weed brownies, and cookies on a regular basis. Normally I'm not one for sweets, but these were very small, and, as I'd find out, packed quite the potent punch.

Opening the first Ziploc bag, a very familiar aroma filled my nostrils. These brownies didn't smell like brownies, they smelled very very ... green.

I put all of them in a tupperware container, and put the container in the fridge to make sure nothing would go bad (and also because, in the highly unlikely event that a police officer were to ever stop by, I didn't want something that reeked of weed to be right there on my kitchen counter).

The Baker gave me a warning, telling me not to eat two brownies, or cookies, back to back. I was to just eat one, no matter how tiny they looked, and wait about half an hour for the effect to kick in.

I ate a brownie, and watched some pro wrestling.

About a half hour later I still wasn't sure if the brownie was having any sort of effect on me. I'm familiar with the feeling of being high (I went to college ... and worked in hip-hop), and my head didn't feel like it was there at this point.

Then I went to get up and go to the bathroom.

Upon standing it became *really* obvious that I was high as f*ck. I damned near felt drunk, but I knew that couldn't be the case unless Stop & Shop was putting something especially "wild" in their wildberry flavored seltzer.

After spending some time with this feeling, my head, and body, were telling me it was time to go to bed, and I slept better than I had in months.

So at this point I knew the baked goods worked for getting me high, the question was what else could they do for me?

I had some prescriptions for anti-nausea meds, but hadn't taken any of them. I read that marijuana was effective at combating nausea, and although I didn't actually throw up at any point, there were many nights when I'd get a feeling like I was going to. It's difficult to describe, but imagine feeling like you have something low in your throat, and you start making the noise like you're going to puke, but it's not nearly as harsh as knowing you're actually going to puke.

It was essentially like the sound a cat makes when it's about to cough up a hairball, except in my case there was no hairball.

This was an issue I dealt with multiple nights per week. It was slightly uncomfortable, but not so much so that I wanted to take a pill for it.

If you haven't noticed, I'm not a big fan of taking pills, especially potentially strong ones. Remember, I ditched the post-operation Oxycodone pills after using just three of them.

During a night when the quasi nausea feelings came up again I went to the fridge and got myself a weed cookie. My friends, I am not kidding when I say the nausea feeling was gone within 20 minutes. Not only that, as a bonus, I was knocked out within two hours.

I know some of you may be wondering why I was so excited to have something that made me sleep. The assumption is chemo wreaks havoc on a person's body, and makes them tired. While this is true, and I was pretty useless after 4pm on most days, your body being tired, and actually being able to sleep, are two very different things.

For example, you can be exhausted, but if you're in pain, or you're nauseous, or you simply feel weak, there's a pretty decent chance that sleep is going to be difficult, or you're only going to get it in spurts, rather than enjoying a good night of rest.

Because I was working out, I was able to combat the feelings of fatigue better than most, but sleeping through the night was still difficult at times for all the reasons mentioned. Having just one weed brownie, or cookie, changed all that. I was able to sleep through the night, and wake up feeling refreshed.

I know none of this is scientific, but I know my body, and I know this version of medical marijuana worked wonders for me. I'm incredibly thankful for The Baker, and have told them this numerous times.

The next time someone wants to debate the effectiveness of medical marijuana, now you know at least one person it worked for, and if you're someone who holds any sort of position in the government, and you're reading this, please make it easier for people to get medical marijuana. This is a life improving drug for cancer patients, and I'm sure many others. We're not out here trying to reenact our favorite Cheech & Chong movies while in the chemo unit ... although if given the chance, *Up in Smoke* would be my first choice ("Hope you're not busy for about a month").

CHAPTER 29:
WORK WORK WORK
WORK WORK

Two of my favorite nicknames that have been bestowed upon me by editors during my career are "The Deadline Assassin," and "The Professional" (thank you Monika, and Manny!). In my mind, a deadline isn't when an article is due, it's *the very last moment* you can turn in an article, and I've always been about handing my work in early. Not only does it reflect better on me, it gives editors more time to look things over, and, as long as nothing needs changing, it gives my editors one less thing to worry about.

A little trick I learned during the times I've been an editor is to give writers a deadline that's really a few days before the actual deadline. This way when the inevitable, "I need a little more time" email arrives, it's really no problem.

With my Type A work personality in mind, I was determined to not let chemo change my pace when it came to my writing (with the exception of the fact that I'd made the decision to not attend concerts while on chemo, and, in turn, not do any in person interviews). I had four weekly columns to write, plus feature length interviews to conduct (done via phone, and email), as well as album, song, and video premieres to book. I was a busy dude!

Staying busy with work provided me with a few things

1. It provided me with money

Hey, even with insurance I had no idea what would be going on with my medical bills, so I figured stacking some extra funds wouldn't be the worst idea in the world.

2. It provided me with a sense of normalcy

There's that word again – normalcy.

It's incredibly important to keep some semblance of your routine when you're going through something like chemo. For me, writing articles – along with going to the gym – was my "normal," and I wanted to keep it up as much as humanly possible.

Believe it or not, some of my most productive weeks occurred while on chemo. I would bring my laptop in, get myself hooked up to my drugs, and start booking phone interviews for when I'd be home, as well as email interviews that I could think up the questions for while in chemo. I also edited like crazy while in that chemo chair.

There was one day, I remember this well, that my editor told me a feature of mine was going to go up a few days early because someone else had flaked on handing something in (my whole "get everything in before the deadline" ideology saved the day!). I had to laugh, and mentioned to the editor that she had to be tempted to tell the writer in question, "The guy going through chemo handed his stuff in, what's *your* excuse?"

3. It provided me with a purpose

For all the "get your rest" folks out there, do you know how incredibly boring life would be if all you did was rest? Sure, my body was going through some serious stuff due to the chemo, but I wasn't about to just sit there like a lump and watch various daytime programs. Instead, I went into booking overdrive.

I started hitting up publicists about artists and entertainers that I might have felt were a little too big for the site I was writing for, but f*ck it, I was in this chair, and I was determined to make something big happen.

Then something big happened.

After months of attempts, I finally booked someone from the TV show *Pretty Little Liars* – Brendan Robinson, who played Lucas.

This was a huge one for me, as PLL was a phenomenon, and I knew the interview was going to be shared heavily by the fan base. Also, it turned my watching of PLL into less of a "guilty pleasure" and more of a, "I'm doing it for work." (FYI, I said the same thing about *The O.C.* back in the day when I interviewed an actor who had a story arc on the show. The whole "I'm doing it for work" thing doesn't explain why I watched *every episode* of both shows, but I digress)

The interview went really well, and the feature was a hit. It was something I could hang my hat on – during chemo I booked an actor from one of the hottest shows on cable TV, and turned it into a damned good, and incredibly popular, feature.

4. It provided me with a heck of a tag line for my cover letter

On all the cover letters I sent after completing chemo I noted that I'd gone through nine weeks of intense chemo treatments and never missed a deadline.

Amazingly, that line didn't get a single reply, but I'm still ridiculously proud of my accomplishment.

CHAPTER 30: VIDEO KILLED THE RADIO STAR

With all the status updates, and pictures, I'd been posting receiving a really great reaction, on April 29th – which was the Saturday before my final full week of chemo treatments – I decided I wanted to show myself in an even more up close and personal form via a video.

I felt that with a video my friends and family who didn't see me at the gym could get a better idea of how I'm doing, hear how I sound, and understand that I was still the jovial warrior I've always been. It would be my way of letting everyone know that, despite the circumstances, I'm still me, and I hadn't lost an ounce of my spirit.

I wrote up a quick script to remind myself of what I wanted to talk about. My checklist included thanking everyone for their support, letting folks know where I was in the chemo process, telling everyone about the bracelets my buddy had made, letting everyone know when I'd be back in NYC again, and doing a quick "sun's out, guns out" at the end, because I'm a meathead with a master's degree, and I love having fun embracing my "meathead" side.

Basically, the gist of everything was to let the world know, "I am kicking cancer's ass."

I posted the video, which ended up just under six minutes in length, figuring maybe a couple hundred friends would have the time to check it out. Hey, everyone's busy, I get that, and quite a few folks still saw me at the gym on a regular basis, or called, or texted.

I woke up the next morning to see well over a thousand people had viewed the video, and there were a bevy comments waiting for me.

Within 48 hours the video had over 2,500 views, and over 100 comments.

Once again, I was floored by the support my friends were showing me. I was also happy I made the decision to continue to be so public about my fight, as each time I told everyone about what was going on, the support I received made me feel like a boxer with the most cornermen in history.

With each post, another person, or two, or twelve, added themselves to my corner, until it felt like an entire arena was rooting me on, and pushing me forward.

If I hadn't already been so determined to keep being a warrior in the face of cancer, I definitely would have felt inspired to continue to be that way for my friends and family.

In the video, when I spoke about the bracelets I made an offer many people couldn't refuse – I said I'd save some for folks I'd see once I was done with my treatments, and that if anyone wanted one mailed to them, I was well enough to go to the post office to mail a few out.

A few turned into A LOT, as a number of friends took me up on the offer.

For an afternoon, my office became a shipping envelope stuffing, and labeling, plant, with me being the foreman, and only worker! I was cool with it, because every time I addressed another envelope I could feel the love. These people actively wanted to show their support, and it was a beautiful thing.

Of course, it wasn't so beautiful for the people who were behind me in line at the post office.

With over a dozen packages in the bag I was carrying, I knew I'd be getting the stink eye from everyone who just wanted to mail a few things.

There was a grandpa type behind me, and he only had a few letters to mail. I told him to go in front of me, because I'd be a while. He thanked me, and while I felt a little bad that I couldn't do that for everyone, I had to get my stuff mailed at some point!

While the postal worker and I were weighing, and pricing, everything I was telling him my story. He must have been a little inspired, as well, as he worked some magic when it came to the package I was sending to The Netherlands (a big shout out to my friend The Dutch Guy. We managed to get one to ya!).

I'd leave with the knowledge that the bracelets would be all over the country, and the globe, within the week, and a receipt so long it rivaled when CVS spits out a dozen coupons for buying a bottle of water.

A very cool aspect of the bracelet mail out was that I'd learn about their arrivals via photos, and even a video, posted by friends.

I appreciated every post. A few were especially moving.

* My old college roommate posted a pic of he and his daughter rockin' the bracelets.

* A friend going through some medical issues of her own used the slogan on the bracelet – stay strong and have faith – to help her get through her own situation.

* Another buddy ended up experiencing one of his children having to fight cancer, and after wearing the bracelet in support of me, he gave it to his child to wear. (Yeah, that one makes my eyes well up a bit too)

So not only did the bracelet work wonders for me, it became a pay it forward type of deal involving personal strength.

That's a truly beautiful thing.

An interesting side note to this – my karate instructors are also divers, and the bracelet I gave to Nancy, which she put around her ankle, has now been on hundreds of dives. How cool is that?

CHAPTER 31:
THE FINAL COUNTDOWN

The Saturday before my final chemo treatment my CrossFit trainers presented me with a gift – a t-shirt that said "Straight Outta Chemo."

I loved it, and wore it to my final chemo treatment.

The final treatment was a celebration, of sorts, as it would be the last time I had to be hooked up to the IV machine and have drugs dripped into me on a Monday morning. That said, I didn't want to celebrate *too* hard, as I fully realized everyone else in the room was on their own journeys, with some, sadly, having their endings already written, as they were terminal.

It was still a decidedly joyous occasion for me, although I was pretty sure the nurses were all going to miss me, and my daily "fuck" outburst when they poked me with the needle.

I don't even remember what I did the rest of that day, I just remember that a week later I was told my white blood cell count had rebounded to the point where I could use public transportation, and attend concerts, without fear that a random sneeze could send me to the ER.

That was the best news I could possibly hear. It had been over two months since I'd been to a concert. For a guy who normally sees well over 100 live acts per year, that was an eternity.

Two nights later I was in the city. In a weird coincidence, my friend Anna Rose had another show, which made her my final show before surgery, and my first show after chemo. This show would also mark my first drink post-chemo (a Fat Tire ale at Rockwood Music Hall).

Even though I was told I didn't have to worry about germs, I was still a bit jumpy whenever I heard someone cough, or sneeze, and viewed the pole I was holding on the 6 train as dirtier than a stripper pole ... then I remembered strippers clean their poles on a regular basis, so that comparison didn't make a lot of sense.

The concert was early-ish − at least early for me − which was good, because my body still wasn't ready to be up *too* late. In fact, I'd find out over the course of the next few weeks that midnight was a definite "I'm done" point for a little while. Hey, that's still *way* better than 4pm, which was my "I'm done" point during chemo.

It would be about a month before I could handle being up until 3am again.

What was important was that I was out there, I was back at shows, and I was listening to my body when it told me it was time to shut it down for the night.

Even weeks after chemo, you still need to recognize your body is the ultimate boss of you, at least for a little while longer.

CHAPTER 32:
THE SHIRTLESS SELFIE

I am not normally one to post shirtless selfies on social media (try to say that five times fast ... especially if you're whoever is doing the audiobook version of this. C'mon, five times fast. I dare ya!).

Maybe I engaged in this behavior back in the Myspace days, but in my 30s I mainly took those types of pictures to keep a track record of how my workouts were going. Also, let's face it, having really nice abs is fun, dammit! I was down to 10% body fat, and that's something to be proud of.

All that being said, I took a shirtless picture of myself the day after I completed chemo. I wanted a visual record that I did, in fact, go beastmode throughout chemo, and only lost two pounds the entire time. Also, this would be the last time I was basically completely hairless (I'm a gorilla, normally).

I told a few friends about the picture, and they suggested posting it, as it would be ... wait for it ... here comes that word again ... an *inspiration* to others.

I thought about this for a few days, and when I realized they were right, I decided to post the picture, with the following note

I was hesitant about being one of those guys who posts a shirtless pic, but after 9 weeks of chemo I want to prove a point ...

This is dedicated to everyone who's said I've inspired them with my determination throughout the process. Even if no one had been watching I still would have gone hard, but knowing people cared, and were inspired, definitely pushed me to get those extra reps in, and rebound quicker from fatigue.

This is dedicated to everyone I worked out with during the process. Thank you for knowing when to push me, and, in a few cases, telling me to slow the f*ck down.

This is dedicated to the a**hole doctor I DIDN'T use who claimed I'd be "off my feet" for two months. Really doc? Cool diagnosis, bro.

This is dedicated to the doctor I AM using, who said I SHOULD keep working out, and credited my health going into this as a prime reason for why I handled chemo so well.

This is #BeastmodeToBeatCancer #MakingCancerTapOut and #BaldAndBadass.

This is #ChemBRO.

To everyone reading this, if you're ever feeling like a path is difficult, if I can maintain this while going through chemo, you can accomplish all of your goals. Just block out any negativity, and embrace your own beastmode.

FYI – I took this picture one day after my final chemo treatment (and yes, I have my own concert photography up in my bathroom. LOL!).

There was a huge reaction to the post, as my friends were right, people were inspired by it.

It is the *only* shirtless pic of me on social media!

CHAPTER 33:
ON MEMORIAL DAY WE MURPH

In CrossFit boxes across America there's a tradition that on Memorial Day we do Murph. Murph is one of CrossFit's Hero WODs (workout of the day). All of the Hero WODs are named after those who've given their lives in service of the country, and they're all incredibly difficult workouts.

Murph was named after Navy Lieutenant Michael Murphy, who was killed in Afghanistan in 2005. The workout consists of

1 mile run
100 pull ups
200 push ups
300 air squats

1 mile run

All while wearing a 20 pound weight vest.

Sounds crazy for anyone to do, right, let alone someone who is exactly two weeks removed from chemo.

Leading up to Memorial Day I started thinking of goals for myself. Finishing Murph was one of them. I'd finished Murph the previous year, but didn't remember my time. I knew that if I could finish it this year it would be a huge accomplishment.

As the day grew near I thought that just finishing it wasn't going to be enough. I needed an even bigger goal to go with it. So with an initial goal to complete Murph, I gave myself a secondary goal of completing it in under an hour.

To answer your next question – yes, I'm batsh*t insane.

I filled up my vest with weights, strapped it on, and when the clock went 3 ... 2 ... 1 ... I was off and running.

Being that we were allowed to break up everything except for the one-mile runs, after I completed the initial mile I opted to do ten sets of 10 pull ups, 20 push ups, and 30 squats. One, because ten is a nice easy number to break everything up by, and two, because I really suck at math and didn't want to have to think too much while doing this workout.

There are times in life when I enjoy deep contemplation – admission, sometimes that deep contemplation is about the nuances of nu-metal – but when doing something like Murph, thinking can be your worst enemy.

The pull ups weren't a problem. The push ups, however, began to get brutal, as the weights in the back of my vest would bounce off my lower back during each rise off the ground.

I tried my best not to check the time, and, quite frankly, it was easy to ignore the clock while pushing myself to get through everything, and with so many people rooting each other on while trying to not pass out.

Again, this was a time when, after the fact, people told me they saw me doing it, so they knew they couldn't quit.

I took a glance at the clock before taking off for my final mile run. I thought, "OK, I may not quite get this entire thing done in under an hour, but I'm gonna make it close!"

The first half mile was tough. The second half mile was damned near impossible. I wasn't running, or even walking, so much as I was dragging my body back to the gym. My friend Andrew, who was on his closing mile run, as well, gave me a, "Good job, man. You're almost there," which inspired me to pick up the pace from one legged zombie, to two legged zombie, and when I spied the garage door entrance of the gym I may have even ratcheted it up to "jogging zombie."

Crossing the finish line, I looked at the clock.

58:51.

I'd completed Murph, exactly two weeks after my final chemo treatment, in 58 minutes and 51 seconds.

I was elated. I was empowered. I was f*cking exhausted!

After everyone was done — we didn't all start at the same time — we were all on the ground in various stages of "completely f*cking done." My trainer, Chris, who'd helped me all throughout chemo, was sitting with his back against the wall, drink in hand. He turned to me and said, "I have no idea how you did that in under an hour just two weeks after chemo."

That was a compliment I wore like a badge of honor.

CHAPTER 34: BECOMING MASTER BERNARD

A few days after Murph I was back in NYC for two concerts, Cosmic Coronas at Arlene's Grocery, and The Motor Tom at Mercury Lounge.

Both shows were great, and The Motor Tom – who I've known for years – even gave me a shout out on stage, although not by name, as they didn't know if I'd want to be singled out as "the cancer guy," which was nice.

Also, small admission here – as the clock was nearing 11pm that night, I started getting tired. My concert going stamina wasn't quite all the way back yet. I actually took a seat off to the side (Mercury Lounge has seating along the walls) with a handful of songs left in The Motor Tom's set. It would be a few more weeks before truly late nights could happen again.

After those concerts it was back to the business of being in the dojo, because while Murph had been on Monday, my fifth degree black belt test was that Sunday.

Again, yes, I'm batsh*t insane.

My father swung by my place at around 7am to pick me up, as we were headed up past Hartford for the test (did I mentioned we were BOTH testing for fifth degree black belt? Yeah, don't mess with the fam, yo!). Fred Villari's only does black belt tests twice per year in the state of Connecticut, and they're always way the heck up in the middle of nowhere.

No, it's not so they can easily hide the bodies of the people who don't make it through the test ... at least, I don't *think* that's the reason.

I was going into this test with a weird limitation that I couldn't avoid – my doctor said I still wasn't allowed to be hit, or hit others.

Now, I want to say right here that I really tried my best to adhere to this rule, but this was a black belt test, and many of the people I was testing with were people I'd known anywhere from 15 to 38 years, so there were times when the rules were thrown out the window. This happened, most notably, near the end of the test – which lasted over four hours.

As with most black belt tests, the proctors love to end everything with sparring. There's something about working everyone to exhaustion, and then having them duke it out, that brings them great enjoyment.

One of my instructors came racing to me before the sparring was set to begin, telling me a younger black belt candidate from our studio was incredibly distraught having realized he left his sparring gear at home, and could he borrow mine?

I said sure, I wasn't planning on using the gear. I wasn't allowed to hit, or be hit (even though both had happened more than a few times already).

After lending my gear to the young man who needed it, my instructor returned, and said, "You can spar, just stand a bit further away from people."

My reaction was loud, and priceless.

"But you just gave away my gear!"

At that moment I became the only person who would be sparring without any gear on. Yes, the guy who had just finished chemo would be sparring ... *without any gear on*!

Guess how long the whole "stay a little further away from people" thing lasted?

It lasted until I wanted my first point. (in sparring, a point is when you score a hit on someone)

After that point IT. WAS. ON.

I don't remember how long sparring lasted, or how many opponents I faced, but at the end I was sweaty, exhausted, and truly felt like I had earned my rank, which was awarded to me (and everyone else in my group, including my father) at the very beginning of the post-test rank advancement ceremony.

The belt came in a nice black box. I slid it open to reveal the black belt with five red stripes.

This was mastery level. This was something I'd worked over 30 years for, and I didn't let a cancer diagnosis, surgery, or chemo, prevent me from achieving it.

Everyone was taking pictures afterwards, and I took a few with my instructors, my favorite being one where I'm ripping open my gi top like Superman to reveal the "Straight Outta Chemo" shirt.

I'd gone from straight outta chemo, to straight into my fifth degree black belt, with a little Murph in-between. Disney couldn't have written a happier ending.

That happy ending, however, would be short lived, as the results of my follow up CAT Scan the next day would immediately place another hurdle in my path, and, in turn, I would need to find another fitness related goal for myself.

PART II
A SECOND HURDLE

CHAPTER 1:
THE FOLLOW UP

I really wanted to end this book on the high of earning my fifth degree black belt. It was, quite literally, a storybook ending. Life, however, likes to throw us curveballs, and one thing I've learned over the years is how to hit a curve (metaphorically speaking. I can't actually hit a curveball to save my soul).

The day after my black belt test I was scheduled for a follow up CAT Scan, just to make sure that everything looked the way it was supposed to. Also, because nothing's better than following an athletic accomplishment with being forced to fast for an entire morning.

Side Note – I have become quite the expert at being the subject of a CAT Scan. I know the entire routine, including when, and for how long, I have to hold my breath. And yes, I do feel that being exposed to that much radiation, I should have a superpower at this point. I haven't developed one, however, so as of now I'd just be a guy in a cape and tights.

Back on the subject of that particular CAT Scan, when I received the results from Dr. Duda they were slightly troubling. He told me that while the chemo worked, and I was in remission, the tumor decided to stick around.

Apparently, in some cases the actual tumor will become resistant to the chemo, even while the chemo is killing all the cancer in it. This was the case for me.

A few options were presented to me, including surgery. Not wanting to go under the knife again, I asked a whole bunch of questions, and eventually learned that as long as the tumor wasn't growing I could sidestep surgery.

Just to be on the safe side, I asked for some surgeon recommendations, and set up an appointment with one to learn more about what the surgery would entail, but in the back of my mind I figured I'd just leave this stupid tumor alone as long as it wasn't hurting me.

My doctor recommended we do another CAT Scan in September, and we continued my monthly blood tests.

While the blood tests all went well, I would not be a fan of the results of the CAT Scan.

CHAPTER 2:
LIKE A SURGEON

Knowing that surgery could be necessary in a worst-case scenario, I set up an appointment with the first surgeon that was recommended, we'll call him Dr. Y, who was located in New Haven.

Dr. Y was highly credentialed, so I was hoping for the best when I met him in late June. Unfortunately, instead I was witness to one of the biggest egos, and worst bedside manners, imaginable. You know what they say about a famous person who begins to believe their own hype? This guy had clearly heard people praise him, and let it go to his head.

I brought my father with me for the appointment to ask any questions I might forget to ask, and to jot down notes I may miss.

Before we saw the doctor we were brought into a room where we waited ... and waited ... and waited. Eventually two assistants came in, they asked me all the "we're filling out a form you've filled out a thousand times before" questions, and then left the room to get Dr. Y.

Again, we waited ... and waited ... and waited.

We nearly called it quits and left, but just as we were saying, "We'll give this guy five more minutes, and then we're leaving," he showed up.

He proceeded to ask zero questions, and drew an example of what would be done during the surgery. I was both shocked, and depressed, at what I saw. They were going to have to make three cuts under my left arm, and in addition to removing the tumor they were going to have to remove up to half of my left lung.

The surgery would require at least one night in the hospital, and, obviously, some recovery time for the stitches to heal and for me to get my breathing back to normal, which I was assured it would.

It was insane to me that *after* surgery for testicular cancer, and *after* three rounds of aggressive chemo, cleaning up what was leftover was somehow more invasive than anything else in the entire process.

Also, I'd never stayed in a hospital overnight, and, quite frankly, it wasn't something I wanted to do.

As I was attempting to wrap my mind around the idea that I kicked cancer's ass, but now potentially had the worst surgery of my life ahead of me, like all the doctors who only viewed me as a medical chart, Dr. Y started talking about how I'd heal, and when I could get back to my life, without actually asking me a single thing about my life.

This guy was what I refer to as a textbook doctor. He had all the textbook answers ready, but didn't understand that every person is different. Quite frankly, I'm not sure he cared. I think he felt his job was to cut people open, fix what's wrong, and sew them back up. We weren't people to him, we were humans, and notches on his medical belt.

I wasn't a fan, but he was viewed as the best, and I could excuse poor bedside manner for greatness. Also, in my mind, I was only interviewing surgeons as a precautionary measure. Actually getting the surgery done was the furthest thing from my mind.

What's that old saying about ignorance being bliss? I was living it at that moment.

Thinking this guy would be fine in a worst-case scenario, I was ready to make my way home – then came the comment.

My dad likes to reach into a doctor's emotions a little bit whenever leaving one of these meetings, and he usually does this by attempting to create a personal connection. As he reached over to shake Dr. Y's hand, my dad said, "I'm trusting you with my son's life." The doctor smiled really big and replied, "You're making the right decision," and then turned around and walked away.

There was no, "I understand, this is really big," or, "We know how difficult it is to deal with this," it was all ego. I legitimately thought there was a chance my dad was going to punch him, and was impressed he held back.

We didn't hold back for long, however, as after we found our way out of the building I don't think we took more than ten steps before we each said, "We aren't using that guy."

CHAPTER 3:
A WARPED WAY OF DEALING

Some people spend all their time worrying when they may have to deal with a major surgery in their near future. I put the entire thing out of my mind, instead focusing on how freakin' great it felt to be healthy, and allowed to be back in large crowds again.

One of my favorite large crowds every year is Warped Tour, and I had my press credentials all set, and my health in order, so I couldn't wait to make the drive down to Long Island in early July to cover the show. GWAR was one of the headliners, and this would be the first time I'd see them live.

I put on a very special t-shirt for the day. My friend Robert Smith (no, not the frontman for The Cure, and no, not the former running back for the Minnesota

Vikings) had created a "Gratitude" tee that said "Gratitude Always Wins," and he made a unique one-of-one for me in Mets colors (we're both Mets fans) while I was going through chemo, saying he loved the way I was handling everything, and felt that I embodied the message. I was honored, and received quite a few compliments on the shirt while at Warped Tour.

As per norm, I had my list of bands I wanted to see, and after getting a copy of the schedule of which acts where on which stages, and when they were performing (Warped Tour usually has upwards of 60 bands on up to 9 different stages, and lasts from late morning until after the sun goes down), I pieced together my personal schedule for the day.

The day ended up sunny, and gorgeous, and I bumped into a number of friends, colleagues, and bands I knew personally. I even ran into an old high school buddy who runs the indie record label Asbestos Records (sup Flood!), and we headed out to the parking lot with a few folks to grab some drinks in-between bands. He joked that I'm the only person he feels is allowed to continually post about workouts, because I did them while going through chemo.

At the end of the day, as I was making my way into the photo pit area for GWAR, who were one of the headliners, and therefore performed last, I noticed a few photographers putting on rain ponchos (I'm not a photographer, but a press pass is a beautiful thing). Rain wasn't in the forecast, but since this is GWAR we're talking about, fake blood was. I wondered if the ponchos were overkill, figuring the fake blood was meant to spray on the actual crowd, not the people who were two feet from the stage.

After the first beheading – yes, I realize that's a fantastic way to start a sentence – it became clear the poncho people knew something. I attempted to dodge the red spray, but it was impossible. I could feel it dripping down my arms, and bolted from the photo pit to the back of the crowd in order to see the rest of the show in a spray free area.

As I enjoyed the rest of their heavy metal alien-based anarchy I wondered what would happen if a cop pulled me over and saw me with what looked to be quite a bit of blood on me. Would he understand, or would I be going directly to jail? I imagined a situation where I was trying to explain, "Officer, I swear, this isn't REAL blood. Just look at the pictures I took and you'll see it's from the antics of a group of heavy metal playing aliens!"

Thankfully, I did not get pulled over, as I'm guessing my very real reasoning would have led to me immediately being thrown in jail, or the looney bin.

A few days later I bumped into a buddy of mine at CrossFit who's a police officer and told him about my imagined situation, and he told me I probably could have just said, "GWAR," and even if the cop didn't know of the band I'd be good.

While Warped Tour was a great time, in a few days I'd go from heavy metal and fake blood, to my next visit with a surgeon. I guess there was a blood theme to the week.

CHAPTER 4:
SECOND VERSE SAME AS
THE FIRST

With the meeting with surgeon number one having given me a pretty negative view of what surgery would entail, my dad and I made our way to the next recommended surgeon, we'll call him Dr. Q.

Dr. Q was far more local than the previous surgeon, but I still wasn't really amped about the idea of surgery. I mean, who is? You'd think with surgeons knowing they're meeting people who have reached their worst-case scenario they'd have some training in dealing with people, but it seems as though communications classes are in short supply at medical schools.

As we waited in the room Dr. Q shared with another doctor at the hospital – a room that featured a magazine rack filled with various entertainment rags that were so old the majority of the relationships on the covers were all over – I was hoping for, actually I was *expecting*, a far better meeting than the one I had with the previous surgeon.

Dr. Q walked in after a few minutes and then did something so remarkably stupid I couldn't believe it.

You know the old saying that you don't get a second chance to make a first impression? The first impression Dr. Q gave us could be summed up in three letters – WTF.

He started things off by saying he noticed we'd seen Dr. Y, and that he loves Dr. Y, and his entire family uses Dr. Y.

WTF? I wanted to shout, "Do you not understand why we're here? We're here because we want a second opinion. We're here because we didn't like Dr. Y. We wouldn't be talking to you if we liked that guy!"

I was flabbergasted that a doctor could be so dense as to start an appointment with a shout out to the doctor we clearly didn't want to use, and basically try to sell us on him.

The rest of the meeting with Dr. Q went much like the meeting with Dr. Y. Apparently all lung doctors are taught how to draw lungs, and I was given another artist's rendering of what would happen to me if I elected to get the surgery. Again, three cuts under the arm. Again, at least one night in the hospital. Again, a projected rehab time, although at least Dr. Q recognized I was in shape, and noted that I'd be back on my feet quicker than most.

I left having essentially danced the same dance with two different surgeons, and felt like as long as surgery wasn't required I wouldn't be doing it.

My September CAT Scan was looming large.

What did I say earlier about ignorance being bliss?

CHAPTER 5: PLAY BALL!

I'd reached a point where I'd become sick of meeting with doctors, sick of being in windowless rooms in hospitals, and sick of being told about how my lung would be cut open.

It was summertime, and I'd already had a taste of medical freedom by going to Warped Tour, and I wanted more. I needed to enjoy the great outdoors.

FYI – my version of "the great outdoors" is a ballpark. Very little in this world makes me as happy as attending a baseball game on a sunny day.

Because I'd spent most of the spring getting chemo treatments, I'd been unable to attend any games. Large crowds are problematic for a person with next to no white blood cells. A simple sneeze from someone five rows up could've sent me to the emergency room.

Thankfully, my white blood cell count bounced back up to normal after I'd completed chemo, and thanks to a generous gift from my friends Jennifer and D'Arcy, I ordered tickets for myself and my parents to a Hartford Yard Goats game. Hey, if anyone deserved an afternoon of fun, sun, and baseball it was the two people who'd gone through the most intense of emotional roller coasters because of my sickness (hey mom, I found a roller coaster you don't like! Sorry!)

My parents had been absolute rocks (and I mean that in a good way). I'm still thankful for how they both put up an incredibly strong front, and only showed an unwavering belief in my ability to kick cancer's ass, while on the inside they were probably experiencing every horrible emotion possible.

Forget surgery, THIS was what the doctor ordered ... for *all* of us!

record scratch

freeze frame

Voiceover: The doctor would order more than just baseball

We had great seats, and of all the ballparks I've been to – which is likely somewhere between 15 and 20 if you combine MLB and MiLB ballparks – it was one of the best ballpark experiences of my life. Seriously, there were so many kind, helpful people there, it felt like we'd been dropped in the middle of the midwest.

My father and I started going to games in upstate Connecticut way back in the day, when the Hartford Yard Goats were in New Britain. Originally they were the New Britain Red Sox, which is when we discovered them. They then became the Hardware City Rock Cats, who eventually changed their name to the New Britain Rock Cats.

As much as I was saddened that they left the New Britain community, I can't argue with how well everything turned out in Hartford.

CHEMBRO

Hey, I bet you didn't expect some random Connecticut minor league baseball history in this book about cancer! If this ever comes up on Jeopardy you're gonna own that category, yo!

CHAPTER 6:
RADIATE GOOD TIMES, COME ON!

On September 6th I had yet another CAT Scan scheduled. This was the follow up to the follow up, as we were looking to make sure the tumor that stuck around like a party guest who didn't know when to leave hadn't grown.

In what seemed to be a routine I had down pat, I was answering all of the radiology tech's questions when she hit me with one that took me a second. She asked the date of my first CAT Scan. I honestly couldn't remember if it had been in January, or February. That's when I heard a voice from behind me say, "It was January!"

I turned around, and the voice was coming from the radiology tech who did my original scan! Clearly I made a heck of an impression on her ... or I was the only person she'd taken care of under the age of a thousand, which, judging by the waiting area, was a distinct possibility.

Lemme tell ya, if you ever want to feel young, the waiting area of a radiology practice is basically a tiny version of a retirement community. It was a stark contrast to Warped Tour, where I was basically old enough to be the father of many of the concert goers (and as all my friends know, I have plenty of dad jokes in my repertoire!).

The tech stuck me with the needle, injected me with the contrast, and I did my best "Machinehead" imitation – breathe in, breathe out, breathe in, breathe out. Come to think of it, why aren't there Bush/Gavin Rossdale themed CAT Scan machines? Talk about a missed branding opportunity!

I went home thinking two things – 1. Hey, the cute radiology tech remembered me, and 2. This CAT Scan will confirm the tumor hasn't grown, and I can go on about my life.

Again, I reiterate – ignorance is bliss.

A handful of days later I started writing the first part of this book. It was September 11th, and quite a few friends had asked me to write up my experience, so I cleared a bunch of time, and typed away.

Three days later, I had written 14k words, and was ready to get my CAT Scan results from Dr. Duda.

CHAPTER 7:
CUT IT OUT

As I arrived at Dr. Duda's office I was hoping for the best. I was hoping he'd say, "Everything stayed the same. Go enjoy life."

Unfortunately, he told me that the tumor had grown, not significantly, but any growth was bad, and we'd reached the point where it had to be cut out.

The sole good news is that the tumor was still small enough to get rid of it via the method the surgeons had told me about, with three cuts under the arm. If I allowed the tumor to continue to grow, the phrase I heard to describe surgery was "crack your chest open," and I was having none of that.

I let Dr. Duda know that I wasn't thrilled with the two surgeons I'd spoken with, and I was going to keep looking. This was when I circled back to Dr. Dowling, the CyberKnife doctor in Stamford who originally recommended Dr. Duda for my chemo. I figured

CyberKnife might be a long shot, but it seemed like my only shot at avoiding surgery.

I called up his office to set up an appointment, and mailed him CD copies of my latest CAT Scans (well, they were supposed to be of my latest CAT Scans, but we were given duplicate copies of the same scan, and had to sort that out), along with a letter explaining why I wanted to see him.

A meeting was set up for the first week in October. At that meeting I heard exactly what I didn't want to hear – surgery was the only option. He even went above and beyond the call of duty to try to help me out, calling up colleagues in NYC to see if there were any experimental programs being run on people my age, but found nothing for anyone who wasn't elderly.

He explained in detail why CyberKnife wouldn't be good for someone my age. From what I took away from the conversation, the procedure almost has a soldering effect inside the body, and while that's fine for older folks, doctors avoid doing it in younger people because it makes future procedures significantly more difficult if they ever have to cut that person open.

Dr. Dowling would turn out to be a hero in this story once again, however, as for the second time he recommended a doctor to us, this time telling us about the thoracic surgeon they have at Stamford Hospital, Dr. Ebright.

To say that Dr. Dowling gave a glowing review of Dr. Ebright would be an understatement. Not only did he say he was a great surgeon, he assured me Dr. Ebright had a much better bedside manner than the other surgeons I'd met, and was a pleasure to deal with.

I left the meeting with Dr. Dowling cautiously optimistic, and hopeful that Dr. Ebright would be the last doctor I'd have to meet on this journey.

CHAPTER 8:
I'M A REAL CUT UP

My meeting with Dr. Ebright was scheduled for two days after my 39th birthday. Some people open gifts on their birthday, I was going to get opened up.

When I arrived at his office, my dad accompanying me, as per norm, I first met Nurse Lauren, whose demeanor, and sense of humor, immediately made me feel like I was in the right place. As I mentioned before, it's really important to have a shared emotional energy with whoever is going to be operating on you, and within minutes it was clear Nurse Lauren was someone I was not only comfortable with, but actually enjoyed being around – the same could not be said for most of the other folks I met with while searching for surgeons for this procedure.

I answered the same million questions I had to answer at every appointment – seriously, every hospital has the same forms, and every hospital has the same set of questions they ask. One humorous moment happened later in the appointment when my answer to, "How many alcoholic drinks do you typically have" was misread as 4 per day instead of 4 per week, which resulted in quite the reaction from all of us when it was read out loud.

When Dr. Ebright walked in the room he greeted us with a smile, and assuring words as to how the procedure would go. Just like the other surgeons, he showed off his surgery art class skills, drawing what would happen.

He also asked me to remove the hoodie I was wearing so he could do a quick check on my breathing, saying I could leave the t-shirt on that I was wearing underneath. I hesitated for a bit. I wasn't nervous about my breathing, I just didn't expect to have to remove my hoodie, so the t-shirt I was wearing under it was a bit off color.

I own a lot of band t-shirts, and this one happened to be for my friends Mother Feather, a rock band in NYC who I'd also met up with at Warped Tour. The shirt features the two female members of the band touching the tips of their tongues to each other.

I warned Dr. Ebright that I was wearing a unique shirt, and I think it became yet another icebreaker in what is normally a situation lacking in humor.

After he checked on my breathing, and said it was perfectly normal, then came the questions ... and not from him – from me!

Unlike the other surgeons I had met with, he was open to hearing all of my questions and concerns – and as a journalist, I ask A LOT of questions.

At one point I apologized for what must have seemed like an in-depth interview, but Dr. Ebright said he actually likes when a patient takes a significant amount of interest in what's going on, and was happy to answer everything. In fact, when I asked how it was possible to cut part of the lung and not lose all the air before stapling it back together, he brought out the actual tools that would be used for the procedure to show them to me.

The instrument that cuts the lung has a stapler on it, so it staples as it cuts. It's really ingenious. It was also a bit larger than I expected. I asked how they could get that in there with just a series of small cuts, but Dr. Ebright assured me it wouldn't be an issue. (side note – looking at the scars, I still have no idea how they fit that thing in there)

I was warned that my breathing would be a bit difficult the first day, but would gradually get better, and I would be back to 100% pretty quickly. He noted that I shouldn't be lifting anything at the gym for two weeks after the surgery, but light cardio would be OK.

Since you're this far into the book you already know what I heard was – cardio is perfectly fine, and I can go back to lifting in two weeks.

After this conversation I didn't need any time to make my decision, I would be using Dr. Ebright for my lung surgery. I told him I'd like to set it up. He suggested Monday. I'm not sure what the look on my face was when he made that suggestion, but I was clearly expecting a much longer timeline.

Wanting to have a bit more time to get my proverbial house in order – i.e. get a bunch of articles written in advance, and clean my *actual* house so I wouldn't have to worry about anything while I was laid up – I asked if it was completely necessary to do the surgery right away?

I knew I had a growing tumor in me, and if he'd told me that waiting any longer would result in my needing a far more invasive surgery, I'd have dropped everything and made the appointment work. Thankfully, he said at the rate the tumor was growing, waiting a few weeks would make absolutely no difference. We set up a few pre-surgery tests for the coming weeks (another CAT Scan, another breathing test, which, ironically, I finally figured out how to knock out of the park just days before having a lung cut into), and scheduled the surgery for November 6th.

I left Dr. Ebright's office confident that I was in good hands, and that although the surgery was my worst-case scenario, I knew I'd be able to handle it.

Now, in addition to doing a bunch of writing, and cleaning, I had to get my head in the right place in regard to my next athletic comeback.

When I didn't think I was going to need surgery, my feeling was I was back to kickin' ass and takin' names, and my road back to beastmode was complete. With this surgery now on the horizon, however, my road back to beastmode was taking yet another detour, or hitting another pothole, or whatever road-based metaphor you'd like to use.

The good news was since I'd made a comeback before, I knew it was possible. I also knew it took time, and I didn't have to attempt to rush things (spoiler alert – I still tried to rush things).

My mindset before was – I must beat cancer, recover from surgery, and train through chemo, so I can test for my fifth degree black belt.

With encouragement from my gym bros, I decided that this time around my goal would be to compete in the coming year's CrossFit Open – the annual event where the overlords of CrossFit announce a new workout every week for five weeks, and everyone competes, and submits their scores. My surgery would be in early November, and the CrossFit Open would come around in late February. Even if I had to scale all the workouts (which is to say, even if I had to scale back the weight, or the moves), I wanted to be able to say I did it.

As I learned from my first surgery, and going through chemo, goals are an incredibly important aspect of the rehab process. You need to be shooting for something, and you need to be shooting for something big, that way even if you fall a little short you're still WAY ahead in the grand scheme of things.

If it turned out that come February I couldn't do the Open, I'd be disappointed, but I'd know I'd be well on my way to being back to 100% because I'd worked toward that goal. With that in mind I gave myself a secondary goal – if it turned out I couldn't compete in the Open, I definitely wanted to do Murph on Memorial Day.

After creating those goals, and putting that level of determination in my head, I was truly ready for the surgery.

CHAPTER 9: PROVING SOMETHING TO MYSELF

While I had my post-surgery goals all set, I still had a few pre-surgery goals I wanted to meet. Basically, I wanted to see exactly how well I'd come back from my previous surgery, and chemo, so I could have even more goals to shoot for, and surpass, once back in action again.

One number I was looking to improve on was my deadlift.

Before my first surgery, and chemo, my one rep max – meaning the most weight I could lift for a single rep – was 315 lbs. I wanted to see if now six months removed from chemo I could better that mark.

Going for a one rep max is quite the process. You build up to your three rep max, and then start doing one reps until you can't lift the bar anymore, or feel you've topped out (or your trainer says your form was really sh*tty, and you shouldn't do it at that weight again). This involves a lot of "lift and wait." You have to give your body time to recover after a super heavy lift, so there's quite a bit of downtime, downtime where you can't allow yourself to get into your own head. You basically have to continually psych yourself up. It helps when there are other people psyching you up, as well, which I happened to have on the Friday before I was scheduled to be cut open again.

As I worked my way up I was feeling good, *really* good. I hit one rep at my previous personal best of 315 lbs, at which point my trainer buddies, and another friend who was there, all commented that the lift at that weight looked easy and I should add tens on each side.

I threw the tens on (not literally. You can't throw plates onto the bar), and psyched myself up. This was going to be a new PR (personal record), and I was going to nail it. My buddy Fred picked up his phone to film the attempt.

After chalking up my hands, I approached the bar, got into the position, and picked that sucker up!

335 lbs! A new personal best just six months removed from chemo, and three days before my lung surgery!

Now that I knew what I was capable of I had yet another goal for after surgery, and recovery – hit 335 lbs again, and then surpass it.

The video of the lift is still somewhere on my buddy's phone, as due to the size of the clip, none of us could figure out how to get it online. Maybe one day we'll figure it out, but we all know it happened, and it was a huge personal boost right before surgery.

CHAPTER 10: CUT MY LUNG INTO PIECES, THIS IS MY LAST RESORT

On the morning of November 6th my parents drove me to Stamford Hospital for my surgery. Did I say morning? I think it was technically pre-morning, as not only was it still dark, and not only was the highway completely clear, there wasn't a single car in any of the patient parking lots at the hospital. Not one!

My surgery was set for 7:30am, but I had to be there closer to 6am to check in, fill out more forms, and get prepped for the surgery. This is where the one and only major issue happened – unbeknownst to me, the hospital had pushed my surgery to 10:30am. All my info said

7:30am, and after a round of fairly pointless back and forth (the surgery was going to be at 10:30am no matter what was on the printouts I'd been handed two weeks earlier) an apologetic representative of the hospital told us it was a screw up on their end, and they would make sure it would never happen again. This is great for anyone else who is going to have surgery there, but I was still stuck there three hours too early.

You might think, "Three hours is a long time. Just go home for a little while." Unfortunately, it was kind of pointless to attempt to go home, because I'd catch rush hour on the way back to the hospital.

Grabbing a bite to eat was also out of the question since I had to fast before the surgery, a fast I started three hours earlier than I needed to because I thought I'd be in the operating room at 7:30am.

All that said, I got over it pretty quickly, and even joked that everyone knows the headliner always goes on stage late, and has to have an opening act.

Eventually I was brought into a room where I stripped down, put on that oh-so-flattering hospital gown, and was stuck with a needle to start running whatever it is they needed to run into me. Oh, and yes, I cursed, cuz that's what I do when I'm stuck with a needle.

As I waited for everything to be ready I was asked the usual questions again, and then I had some of the folks who'd be in the room for the surgery introduce themselves, including one of the doctors, and the anesthesiologist. The latter had a voice for radio, and in my head I wondered why he chose this particular profession ... I figured it out when I received the bill.

I noted that when I had anesthesia as a young teenager I cursed a lot when I was under. He told me that wouldn't be an issue since I'd have a tube down my throat.

Yay?

I asked what would happen if I had to go to the bathroom while I was under. They replied that I'd have a catheter. I was like, "That'll be out before ..." and before I could finish the sentence they said, "It will be out before you wake up." I breathed an audible sigh of relief and said, "Thank God!"

I'd actually have a variety of tubes in me, including one that would remain in after surgery – a drainage tube. This would be the most important tube, as it would determine when I could go home. Dr. Ebright let me know that I *could* have to stay in the hospital for multiple days, as how quickly I drained, or more precisely, *stopped* draining, would be the indicator that I was ready to go home.

I was not thrilled at the news that what I thought was supposed to just be an overnight stay might be extended, but there was nothing I could do about it, so I pretty much nodded, reminded my body of how well I treat it, and told it to get this sh*t handled as efficiently as possible.

When they were given word that the operating room was ready for me I said a few words to my parents, and was wheeled out through the halls, and into one of the most impressive rooms I've ever seen in my life.

I knew my surgery was being done using robotics. I didn't know that the robotics were going to be quite so large.

The room was vast, filled with equipment, and what seemed to be enough people in scrubs to field a baseball team.

They wheeled the bed I was on right up alongside the operating table and told me to slide over onto it. This is actually more difficult than it sounds when hooked up to a bunch of medical equipment, and is a totally ridiculous way of moving from one bed/table to another. I asked, "Can I just get off this bed, and get onto the operating table?" Nope. That wasn't allowed. When I asked why, they didn't really have a solid reason other than it's just the way it's done. I don't know, maybe the floor is lava.

Once I was on the operating table the anesthesiologist hooked me up. I had a few things explained to me about the surgery, things that I'm not sure ever really made it into my head, because immediately afterward the anesthesiologist said he was going to start my drip, at which point I said OK, and I don't remember a thing that happened after that.

CHAPTER 11:
MY LUNG SURGERY
PLAYLIST

As you know by now, I use humor as a way of handling even the most trying times, and scary moments in life. My lung surgery was no exception, as before I left for the hospital I posted my weekly pop column, Pop Shots, dedicating it to my operation by creating my lung surgery playlist.

The column, which originally appeared on Adam's World, and was one of my blog's most read posts of 2017, included a video for all eight songs, with a little write up for each. Here's the complete playlist, with my commentary.

Pop Shots – My Lung Surgery Playlist

Welcome to your weekly dose of pop world musings. As some of you may know, I've had a rough year – testicular cancer diagnosis, surgery, chemo – and this morning I'm going to the hospital one more time to get a tumor, and the section of my left lung it's attached to, removed.

Normal people freak out right before having surgery to remove a section of their lung. Me? I'm all, "Let's make a lung surgery playlist!"

After going through dozens of breathing related songs, and noticing many of them are about not breathing, I decided to make this playlist the complete story of what will be my day.

So check out my lung surgery playlist, and since this is Pop Shots, you know everything is seasoned with a little bit of attitude.

Evanescence – Going Under

While I will, in no way, be "falling forever," I will most definitely be "Going Under" for this operation. Let's just say lung surgery calls for a little more than a local anesthetic.

Until I take that surgery nap, however, you can be sure I will be rockin' out exactly this hard.

Life is a concert, and I crank it up to eleven.

Hooverphonic – Lung

For my surgery I can take the chorus of this song almost completely literally. "Let's open it / Be strong / Cut out / it's lung." Thankfully I'm not losing a full lung, but I'm having part of a lung cut out, so let's just say this one's relatable ... and dope!

Weird Al – Like A Surgeon

I can say with complete certainty that this will not be the very first time my surgeon cuts, but Weird Al has always been a part of the soundtrack of my life, so how could I possibly leave this classic out of my surgery playlist?

Britney Spears – Piece Of Me

My doctors most definitely want a piece of me. Actually, I want them to have that piece of me, as that particular piece has the potential to cause some serious complications in my life. So take that piece of me, medical team ... and then do a choreographed dance routine. I'm sure professional choreography is covered by my health insurance.

The Police – Every Breath You Take

Setting aside the stalker vibe of this song, for me "Every Breath You Take" is totally about how the doctors and nurses will be monitoring my breathing both during, and immediately after, surgery. Every breath I take, they'll be watching me ... because they have to make sure everything went as planned.

Katy Perry – Waking Up In Vegas

While I won't literally be waking up in Vegas, I'll be "waking up in Vegas" in the abstract sense of the phrase. I'll have no idea what happened after blacking out (from anesthesia), I'll wonder how long I was out, and I could quite possibly find myself married to Katy Perry. OK, that last part probably won't happen, but there's always a chance!

Kelly Clarkson – Catch My Breath

In the most literal sense, I will need to take some time to "Catch My Breath" post-surgery. The lung is an organ that heals rapidly, but I'm still gonna have to chill on the intense cardio for a week, or two. As someone who doesn't do "sedentary," this will actually be a bit of a challenge.

Bush – Machinehead

"Breathe in. Breathe out. Breathe in. Breathe out. Breathe in." Gavin Rossdale closes out this playlist giving me some solid post-surgery advice.

And with that, my time is up for the week, but I'll be back next week with more shots on all things pop.

It seems I've referenced "Machinehead" twice in this book now. Shout out to Gavin Rossdale.

CHAPTER 12:
ADVENTURES IN RECOVERY

I don't remember exactly when I woke up, but when I finally opened my eyes again I was in a hospital room, hooked up to more equipment than the back of an old stereo system.

The rooms in Stamford Hospital are actually really nice. It was closer to feeling like a hotel room than a hospital room, although in hotel rooms you're actually allowed to get out of bed.

The nurse on duty informed me about my morphine drip, which I controlled. I was assured that it was impossible for me to overuse it, and that using it wouldn't cause my stay in the hospital to be extended. I'm not sure how they knew that last item was on my mind, but I legit thought that the less I used the morphine the more likely they'd be to let me go. Even with the news that usage wouldn't be an issue, I still didn't plan on abusing it, as I'd rather feel a little pain to know what I'm *not* supposed

ADAM BERNARD

to do than be totally pain free and potentially mess myself up more.

Occasionally that comes back to bite me in the ass, but as a rule it's worked out pretty well for me in life.

Once I had the rundown of what was going on, and that another nurse would be in to get me up and walking around later in the evening, I asked for two pitchers of water (I drink a lot of water), and broke out the protein bars, and protein drinks, I'd brought with me. I'd never stayed in a hospital before, but I'd heard plenty of stories about hospital food, and I knew it wasn't going to be anything like the great meals friends had dropped off at my place for my recovery (thank you friends and neighbors!), so I came prepared.

I'd also brought my Kindle so I could post a few updates on social media letting friends and family know I was out of surgery, awake, and mildly cognizant. Wanna know a secret? I'd pre-written a few of those updates so I could just cut and paste them, as I wasn't sure how woozy I'd be after surgery.

My folks went home, and I watched a little ESPN (shout out to Papi, of *Highly Questionable*, for making me laugh so quickly after surgery).

Because I was hooked up to so many different devices, including that drainage tube, which had a decent sized container attached to it, I had to buzz the nurse every time I needed to go to the bathroom, and boy oh boy are hospitals *super* interested in a patient's bathroom habits.

When I decided it was time to pee, I buzzed the nurse (if you're hoping for a hot nurse story, I'm sorry to disappoint you – the night nurse turned out to be a dude. Even if it had been a beautiful woman, I'm not sure how well I'd have been able to ratchet up the charm while high on morphine, and with a tube

162

coming out of the side of my body). For this time only I was allowed to use the toilet. I fairly quickly realized why this was a special deal.

Being that I'd had a catheter put in, and then taken out, the initial urination wouldn't be 100% normal. Of course, I wasn't warned about this, I just let out an awkward "whoa" midway through going to the bathroom, at which point the nurse asked if I'd fell. I replied, "No, but something strange happened. It felt like everything was going in reverse." He said that's because of the catheter having gone in, and been removed.

That was the last time I was allowed to go to the bathroom using the toilet while I was in the hospital. All other times the nurse on duty would bring in a plastic jug, because they wanted to measure how much was coming out of me. It was actually kind of funny, because I drink so much water, the first time a nurse came in with one jug I was like, "I'm gonna need more than one of these."

Was I absolutely sure about this? No, but being that I was peeing into a jug, next to my bed, and not in a bathroom, I sure as heck didn't want to be wrong and end up peeing all over the floor.

After nearly filling BOTH jugs the nurses seemed impressed (FINALLY, someone who was impressed with what I have going on down there!), and shortly thereafter my nurse got me up and moving, and had me go on my first walk around the floor I was staying on.

The walk actually required a lot more coordination, and teamwork, than one might expect. I had to have a nurse carrying the container the drainage tube was draining into, and never walk any faster, or slower, than I was going, because that tube was a short leash, and it wasn't going to feel good if it was tugged on.

I had to man the IV pole (I'm sure there's a medical term for it, but I'm going with IV pole, and no, there was no pole dancing). This was fine until the flooring changed, or there was a lip in-between areas that I had to get over.

It was really quite the production.

As I was walking, the nurse was asking how I was feeling, and if I could handle walking through another section. My breathing was obviously a bit off, but I felt fine walking around, and told him we could do another lap. After the second lap he told me to take it easy, and that I'd have another walk around the floor in the morning.

At this point I had a very important decision to make – did I want to lay in the bed, or sit in the chair? I chose to sit in the chair, watch *Monday Night RAW*, and call a few friends. My friends Bear, and Amy, had the exact same reaction when they heard my voice – "You don't sound like someone who just had surgery."

Apparently I sounded like I always do, which led to some fantastic assumptions about my level of toughness.

After *RAW* was over I paged the nurse to help me get back into bed. Once in bed I had some funky cuffs put around my calves that would inflate, and deflate, at intervals throughout the night. Basically, they wanted to keep the blood flowing, knowing I wasn't going to be able to roll over, or move at all, while sleeping.

Even with the morphine drip, sleep wasn't easy. Not only was I hooked up to machines that beeped, a hospital, even at its most quiet, is still filled with unfamiliar noises. It's crazy, I live by a fire station, so I'm used to hearing fire trucks drive by with their sirens blaring, but a printer being used, or steps down a hallway ... *that's* gonna keep me up at night.

There was also something else totally unexpected that kept me up – hospital alarms, and pre-recorded emergency messages.

You see, while my room was really nice, I was at Stamford Hospital during their massive renovation/rebuild, and while I was there, in the middle of the night a machine hit a pipeline outside. That set off every alarm because, as I would later find out, it killed the heat in the building I was in.

I heard the alarms, and the pre-recorded message, which was repeated ad nauseum, but it wasn't until my nurse came in – wearing a jacket – to tell me what had happened that I had any idea the heat was no longer working. After breaking the news he asked me if I needed any more blankets. I was such a perfect combination of exhausted, and high on morphine, that I thought everything was fine. Once he said we had no heat, however, it only took about two minutes for me to realize I was freezing. I called him back in, and he brought a couple very warm blankets that helped me get a couple hours of sleep before I was awoken to do another few laps around the hospital floor.

CHAPTER 13: HOMEWARD BOUND

At around 6am it was time to do my laps again, which I completed with ease. When I arrived back at my room Dr. Ebright stopped by to see how everything was going, and after taking a look at the container my drainage tube was attached to, he said he'd get someone in here to detach me, and that I'd be free to go home.

I was stoked. The whole "you might be here a couple of days" spiel was just to prepare me for the worst ... or to have me doubly excited when I was told I could leave after one day. Hey, either way I was outta there!

As an aside, another doctor that I'd met earlier in the process – Dr. Drummond – also stopped by to see how I was doing, and that meant a lot. I wasn't actually her patient, and she'd only met me once, but she took time out of her day to check up on me, which I appreciated. Unlike the doctors who only viewed patients as a chart, she was a great example of a doctor who really understands that patients are people.

A nurse came by at around 7am to remove the drainage tube. This was an interesting process, and by interesting I mean I had no idea what the heck to expect.

From what I was told, I had some bandages around the tube, holding it in, and a stitch in place, ready to be tied once the tube was pulled.

The nurse removed the bandages as nicely as possible, and then asked me if I was ready for the tube to be pulled out. When I replied that I was, he said, "OK, brace for it. On three ..." In my mind I was like, "Brace for it? How does one brace for this? I've never had a tube   pulled out of me before!" I clenched up a bit, and prepared for what I thought was going to be some truly awful pain. Instead it was just a slight pain, and an overall weird sensation of having something pulled out of my body that wasn't supposed to be there.

Seconds later the nurse had my stitch tied, and I called my dad to tell him the good news.

That's when things started to slow down.

While I was told that after I had some x-rays done I'd be all checked out by 11am, the check-out process for hospitals isn't exactly like the check-out process for a hotel. Hotels want you out of there, so they can get the next customer in the room. Hospitals have sick, wounded, and recovering people to deal with, so dealing with the quasi-healthy folks ranks pretty close to last on their list of important things to handle.

The morning nurse – it was another guy, as I was not given the hot nurse fantasy – came in, and asked me if I wanted one last drip of morphine before they unhooked me. I said I felt fine, figuring I'd be home shortly. Out came the IV, and I was hooked up to one less thing.

The phone rang, and it was the cafeteria telling me they were going to stop serving lunch soon, and wanting to know if I had an order. I told them I was due out shortly, and wouldn't need any food.

Can you see the bad moves mounting up here?

Up next was the removal of the ECG pads that were attached to my chest, and had been hooked up to yet another machine that had been monitoring something.

No problem, right? They're just some round pads.

Ah, but there was a problem, quite the major problem for me – no one shaved my chest before putting the ECG pads on me, and there were quite a few of them.

God bless the nurse for trying his best, but the notion that if you rip the proverbial band-aid off quickly it causes less pain is the biggest load of horse sh*t known to man.

As the nurse tore the first one off I let out a noise I didn't know I was capable of making. It was sort of like a high-pitched whimper, and at that point I gave the nurse my best Heisman pose, indicating I wanted him to stop.

I told him I'd handle the rest, although he did get the one on my back, which would have been impossible for me to reach.

I slowly worked my way around each of the remaining ECG pads, although I was tempted to just wear them until they fell off (I'm not sure the hospital would have been cool with that).

So now I was clear of all tubes, IV lines, and ECG pads. I was just ... waiting, and waiting, and waiting.

Finally, at around 1pm, I was given everything I needed to leave. I was hyped to get dressed, and go home. I ran into a little problem with the whole "getting dressed" part, though. I knew I wasn't going to be able to put a t-shirt on due to the incisions underneath my arm, but that wasn't the big deal, as I'd brought a zip up hoodie. The big deal was that the morphine I'd been taking overnight had worn off while I was waiting, and I could no longer reach down to put on my shoes.

I felt like a child in a shoe store, requiring other people to loosen my shoelaces, and help me put on my shoes.

I then attempted to stand. The pain was ridiculous. Seeing this, the nurse wrangled me two pain pills, and some Jello-O (fun fact – I can only take pills with food. OK, maybe that fact wasn't all that fun, but I know there are a lot of other folks like me out there). The pills were Oxycodone, the same pills I tried my best to avoid the first time around, and gave me horrible constipation. I knew I needed them, though, so I picked them up, and realizing full well it meant that I probably wasn't going to sit on a toilet for about a week, I swallowed both.

Getting into the car was tough, but just 20 minutes later, when my dad and I arrived at my local drug store to pick up my prescription – 30 more Oxycodone, only two or three of which I'd use – I had no problems getting out of the car, and could even squat down to re-tie my shoes.

I didn't like the side-effects of the pills, but good God almighty did I need them that day.

As we walked through the drug store I spoke with a few of the folks who worked there who I've known for years, and when we arrived at my building I knocked on a few neighbors' doors to let them know I was back. The looks I received would be best described as "pleasantly shocked."

Once I was situated back at my place my dad left, and I decided to take the rest of the day off. I felt like I'd earned it. That said, the next day was another story.

I knew I'd have trouble sleeping for a while, as the cuts were on the side of my body that I normally sleep on, but my previous surgery taught me how to get out of bed while dealing with stitches, so I felt like I already had a leg up on the recovery process this time around, so

Wednesday was going to be a day where I started the road back to beastmode.

Yes, that's right, on a day when many assumed I'd still be in the hospital, I'd be taking the first steps to my comeback ... well, technically second steps, the first steps were those laps around the hospital, but doesn't "taking the first steps to my comeback" sound *way* more dramatic?

CHAPTER 14:
WALK THIS WAY

I woke up on Wednesday predictably sore, and completely willing to pop an Oxycodone, although I was going to keep to my plan of not using them for more than a day or two (FYI, I stuck to that plan, and didn't use 27 of the 30 that were prescribed to me).

Once I was able to move easily, I decided it was time to start the rehab process. I was going to surprise some friends at CrossFit by walking over there to say hi, then on the way home I was going to make a stop at the drugstore for an iced tea. All in all, it was going to be around a two-mile jaunt.

My goal was to walk at a decent, but not fast, pace – I traditionally have what my friend K.Gaines calls a "tri-state gait," meaning I walk quickly even when I'm not in a hurry.

Not only was I not supposed to walk fast right away due to the whole having my lung cut open and stapled back together thing, I also didn't want to walk fast because I wasn't allowed to shower until the bandages covering the stitches were removed, and this was something I was told I couldn't do until Friday. That's right, I had to go from Monday, until Friday morning, without a shower.

In lieu of showers, the advice I received from the nurses was to use baby wipes to clean myself. Yes, baby wipes. I wiped myself down in the morning, and again before bed. If there was a woman out there with a fetish for grown men who smell baby fresh, I was that woman's dream man.

I still couldn't put on a t-shirt, so I zipped up my warmest hoodie, and started the two-mile trek. Lemme tell ya, it felt good. Knowing that on a day where I could have still been in the hospital I was out and about, walking around town, was a great feeling.

I said hello to some friends at CrossFit — including my mom, who was there for a workout — and everyone agreed I did not look like a man who'd just had surgery.

After telling them my walking plan I joked with my trainer, Chris, that I wanted to know today's WOD. He said it was for me to walk to the drug store, and then walk home.

At the drug store I found the large bottles of iced tea were on sale as long as you bought two of them. This created a conundrum. I wasn't supposed to lift *anything* for two weeks. Two half-gallon containers of iced tea definitely counted as "anything," but I live right around the corner from the store, so I figured what the heck.

As soon as I turned the corner after leaving the drug store, I bumped into my friend Melissa, who was also out taking a walk. I believe her first words to me were, "What the heck are you doing?" It was a reasonable question.

I insisted that me carrying these bags that each contained a half gallon bottle of iced tea was perfectly fine, but let's face it – your friends know when you're full of sh*t, and while she couldn't have possibly known what my doctor had told me about lifting things, she knew that someone who just had part of a lung removed was probably given more than a few restrictions, and that I was the type to ignore, or at least test the boundaries of, said restrictions.

Persistence on her part led to me giving her my bags to carry back to my place.

I still swear I could've done it and I would've been fine, but I definitely appreciated her help.

The next day I spent a solid 20+ minutes taking the bandage off my side, which required the use of about a dozen small medical towelettes that dissolve adhesive, and about a million gentle tugs at various ends of   the bandages.

Believe it or not, 20+ minutes was actually significantly faster than I'd imagined the process would go. I booked an hour of my day to get that done.

After I'd removed the bandages, and as much of the adhesive as possible – some of it was *really* stuck on, to the point where it took over two weeks to come off – the three cuts where I had dissolvable stitches on the inside were revealed – two on the side, one on my back – as was the lone outside stitch where the drainage tube had been. That stitch was long, and looked a bit like a pull cord, although it would qualify the most painful pull cord in the world.

Now freed from my adhesive-based bondings, I took one of the longest, greatest, most amazing showers I've ever taken in my entire life. For the first time in a week I truly felt clean.

I also got back work, prepping columns, and interviews.

You didn't actually expect me to go a full week without working, did you?

Obviously I was still dealing with some post-surgery pains. Heck, I couldn't even lift my left arm all the way up. The worst pains, however, came when I needed to yawn, or sneeze. With a healing lung, my breathing was less than perfect, and every time I yawned there was a weird hitch in it. I'd start to yawn, pause because my throat would close up, and then finish the yawn. It was the yawn equivalent of Charles Barkley's golf swing.

Sneezing was a literal pain, as not only did I have to get the air for it, having a bunch of stitches in your side makes each sneeze a real treat.

But hey, if that was the worst I had to deal with, I counted myself lucky.

I also counted myself smart enough to know my limits (bag carrying not withstanding).

I'd been invited to see one of my favorite bànds, Larkin Poe, in NYC, but the show was just a few days after the surgery, and with my breathing nowhere near back to normal, I wasn't sure if I should risk the long walk from the subway to the venue, or being in a super crowded place, so I passed. It was a tough decision, but my feeling was I didn't survive cancer and lung surgery just to die on the side of the road walking to a show because I was too much of a dumbass to realize breathing is important. (Thankfully, I was able to see Larkin Poe when they came through the city the following year)

CHAPTER 15:
HIGH MILEAGE

Although I wasn't allowed to lift, I had a pretty solid goal for myself for the remaining week where I could only do cardio – walk more every day than I did the day before, while also slowly but surely improving my pace.

Starting that Saturday I was able to hit the treadmill, although obviously at a reduced speed. Regardless, we're talking about November in Connecticut, so it was nice to be able to walk somewhere a bit warmer than it was outside.

On day one I walked 3.5 miles on the treadmill. This was followed by 4.8 miles, 4.2 miles on a CrossRamp machine, 4.25 miles on the treadmill plus a 2-mile walk, and 4.65 miles at a fairly decent jogging pace.

There was only one issue with all this walking on the treadmill – it was incredibly f*cking boring! (There goes that lucrative treadmill sponsorship. Oh well) Add to that the fact that I was looking at a wall the entire time, and there was a chance I could go crazy.

Because my friends at CrossFit knew this, very early on in the process they printed out a picture of Vanessa Hudgens, wrote an inspirational note under it, and taped it to the wall in front of the treadmill to keep me motivated.

Within just a few days everyone at the gym knew the picture of Vanessa was for me, and it stayed up the entire time I had to use the treadmill (the picture, that is). This is yet another (absolutely hilarious) way friends can play a role in the recovery process.

There's actually a funny clip of me reaching out towards the picture in SOSF's 2017 year-in-review video.

Finally, on the Monday I was scheduled for my follow up appointment with Dr. Ebright, I felt well enough to get on an Assault Bike. I did not use the arm function of the bike, as that was still a no-go until getting the green light from Dr. Ebright, but I could pedal. Oh boy could I pedal, and the bikes faced out into the gym, so I could see people, and have an actual conversation!

I decided I would bike for an hour, non-stop, at a decent, but not crazy, pace.

There was at least one comment about me looking like I was training for the Tour de France, and at the end of the hour I'd racked up 16.6 miles.

I was looking forward to telling Dr. Ebright the news when he asked how I was doing.

CHAPTER 16:
CUT THAT STITCH! CUT
THAT STITCH!

I arrived at Dr. Ebright's office at Stamford Hospital excited at the prospect of good news. I felt like I'd made great progress, and was looking forward to telling him about my workouts.

Nurse Lauren came in first, and asked how I was feeling. I told her about my 16.6 mile stationary bike ride from the day before. She joked, "Only 16.6 miles?"

Dr. Ebright has a similarly great reaction, saying, "That's good. We recommend patients keep it under 18 miles."

Needless to say, it had been well established that I was a crazy person when it comes to working out, and they had no problem having some fun with it.

I had the one outside stitch cut out, and was assured that it would be very difficult to rip the inside stitches, although they noted I shouldn't go out of my way to attempt to do things that could make that happen.

A funny moment happened during the cutting of the outside stitch. I tensed up, and gave a pained, snake-like hiss, at which point Nurse Lauren said, "I haven't even done anything yet!"

Yup, that's right, I tensed up because of cold scissors. Apparently I'm a baby around needles, and cold scissors. What a tough guy!

One major question I had was about a strange feeling just under the area where the incisions were made. Even though I'd taken off the adhesive over a week ago, it still felt like there was adhesive pulling on the skin on that side of my abs. I thought a little adhesive might be leftover, but not so much that it would feel like the entire set of bandages were still there.

It was also still really difficult to look over my right shoulder, especially when pulling out of a parking space. I joked that I checked the mirrors and then said a prayer that no one was in my blind spot.

Dr. Ebright informed me that the feeling I was dealing with wasn't from the adhesive at all. Rather, it was an angry nerve.

In order to do the surgery, one of the instruments involved ends up touching a nerve. There's simply no way to avoid this. Nerves, however, *really* don't like being touched, so I was going to have that feeling for a while, and there was nothing I could do to speed up the recovery process. Nerves take time to heal, and that timetable varies wildly.

What I could, and couldn't do at the gym became a series of experiments. Basically, I did a movement, and if it hurt, I stopped.

The good news is I was cleared to lift again, although, as I'm sure you could guess by now, I was advised to come back *slowly*. I was told to stay the heck away from pull ups, or anything involving hanging from the bar. That was obvious, and not an issue, as I still couldn't raise my left arm all the way up. I was working my way back to being able to do that. Also, and this is another obvious one, I was told not to bench press for at least another month. The lung needed to be fully healed for that, and they really didn't want anything heavy hitting my chest, and potentially screwing things up.

I asked Dr. Ebright if January 1st was a reasonable goal for me to be back at 100%.

Now, I swear that was the way I worded the question, so when he said yes, I was stoked. I'm not sure what I meant, and what he meant, however, was exactly the same.

When I said "be back at 100%," I meant "be back lifting at the same weight I was lifting before surgery." A few weeks, and a few phone calls later, I think what he meant was, "be healthy enough to start getting back to my normal routine."

Basically, I was thinking of January 1st as the end of the recovery, while I think he was thinking of January 1st as the start of seriously building back to where I was.

Of course, I didn't know this at the time, so I left happy as heck, ready to get back to lifting, or at least the lifts that didn't affect the nerve.

CHAPTER 17:
THAT GUY'S GOT SOME NERVE

Back at CrossFit I discussed my recovery goal of being able to compete in the 2018 CrossFit Open come February, even if I had to scale every workout, and my trainer really liked the idea.

As I noted earlier, pull ups were out, as were toes to bar, two of my favorite exercises. Just about anything chest related was out, as well, so I was pretty limited those first few weeks.

While working my way back I learned that deadlifts over a certain weight were also a no-go, and as my trainer pointed out, there was really no point in pushing it, potentially hurting myself, and giving myself a setback in my recovery. Being that he's a chiropractor, he knows a thing or two about nerves, and even warned me that the recovery could take longer than expected.

I took it slow – at least slow for me – and after about two weeks I was starting to feel pretty good. The nerve pain was still there, and I still wasn't going to drive any distances, especially on the highway, while unable to completely look over my right shoulder, but I could feel very obvious progress.

The not going on the highway part was only sad for me in one instance. Every year I'm a sponsor of Joey Batts' Hip-Hop for the Homeless Tour. Batts is an emcee, and teacher, in Connecticut, and for this particular tour he gathers up a bunch of local hip-hop artists, and they perform shows in various cities in CT with all of the proceeds and donations going to a local homeless charity in that particular city.

While I still was a sponsor of the tour, I was unable to attend due to my nerve issue.

That disappointment aside, I was feeling like my recovery was going well, until one morning I woke up with a little soreness in my back, on the left-hand side.

I worked out, as oftentimes all I need is to get moving to feel better, but this time I still felt some soreness afterward.

I was finally able to reach my left arm all the way up again, so I went to the rig, and while standing on the ground I grabbed the pull up bar, just to stretch out my back for a bit. It felt great. Everything seemed to be going fine, until I arrived home and went to reach for a pair of jeans in my closet. I screamed. I was in that much pain. I screamed, and growled, and wondered what the heck was going on.

I called Dr. Ebright's office. When I explained what I'd done they told me that the nerve that had been touched during surgery was actually wrapped around my side, from my abdominal area to ... you guessed it ... my back, and while I thought I was stretching out a muscle, what I was really doing was pissing off the nerve.

They advised me to take it easy, which I did for the rest of the day.

The nerve issue would prove to be my biggest hurdle, as even months later, when I couldn't feel it in normal everyday life, and driving felt fine, it would still make its presence known during the occasional workout, or body movement.

One thing I found that helped out a lot was rowing. There was something about that motion that really made everything feel better. I spent an entire week incorporating rowing into every workout.

As the weeks passed, and we hit the New Year, I started to wonder if I'd be able to reach my goal of competing in the 2018 CrossFit Open. I was still unable to do pull ups, or toes to bar, without pain, and that was a concern for me.

My trainer, Chris, reminded me that with a nerve issue you never really know when it's going to heal.

About a week before the CrossFit Open was set to begin I felt I was close to 100%, and at the very least I'd be able to scale all of the Open workouts. Chris then suggested I not only sign up for the open, but that I write about the experience, as he said he'd read lots of stories about people coming back from injuries to compete in the Open, but he'd never read about someone coming back from cancer to compete.

It was settled. I paid the $20 to sign up, and that Thursday I was glued to Facebook Live for the announcement of the first CrossFit Open workout.

CHAPTER 18:
FROM CANCER TO THE
CROSSFIT OPEN

From Cancer to the CrossFit Open was a six week series of columns I wrote for my CrossFit box – SOSF CrossFit and Chiropractic in Fairfield, CT – about coming back from everything you've read about in this book to compete in the 2018 CrossFit Open.

To give you a gist of what I was doing, why it was important to me, and how it relates to my story, the following are reworked excerpts from those columns with some added commentary.

Background info – CrossFit Open workouts are numbered by the last two digits of the year, followed by the number of the workout, so the first workout of 2018 was 18.1, and so on.

Also, the workouts can be done Rx, which is the prescribed weight and movements, and Scaled, which is scaling down in some way, shape or form. Doing the workouts Rx counts for a much higher score, even if you can do more significantly more reps Scaled.

Week 1 – 18.1

While being among the over 90,000 people watching the announcement of CrossFit Open workout 18.1 online, my main hope was that there wouldn't be anything involving hanging from the pull up bar. I felt like I might be able to do that in a couple weeks, but wasn't sure if I'd be able to make it happen quite yet.

Of course, the first exercise announced was toes to bar, which is where you're hanging from the pull up bar and bringing your toes up to touch it. That was followed by dumbbell clean and jerk (bringing the dumbbell from the ground, or a hanging position, to the shoulder, and then overhead), and rowing.

The latter two exercises I knew I could do, the former I used to do with ease, but I had legitimate concerns about potentially aggravating that nerve again. Stone Temple Pilots once sang, "Take time with a wounded hand, cuz it likes to heal." I found the same ideology applies to wounded nerves.

On Friday morning I decided to see what I could do without hurting myself. I chalked up my hands, and gripped the bar. Not bad. I felt OK. I did a few hanging knee raises, which is the scaled version of toes to bar for the workout. Not much pain at all. I attempted a toes to bar … and there it was, there was the nerve telling me, "Hey, do that again and I'm gonna totally ruin the rest of your day!"

With that, it had been decided, I would be scaling 18.1.

I grabbed a 35 lb dumbbell, and moved a rower near the rig (in retrospect, I probably wasn't going to be lifting the Rx weight of 50 lbs overhead at this point in the recovery process, so scaled was definitely the best option. I guess if the dream of a completely Rx-ed Open was going to die, it's best to have it die the first week, rather than get all the way to week 5, and suddenly have the proverbial rug pulled out from under you).

My buddy Rich Quintans (who was voted Fairfield, CT, personal trainer of the year) set the clock for 20 minutes, and after giving me some words of wisdom about properly pacing myself, IT. WAS. ON.

You know how I said I needed goals for my recovery? I also needed goals for each workout. The ideology was the same – I wanted something to shoot for.

I gave myself a goal of attempting to make it through 10 rounds (each round was 8 hanging knee raises, 10 dumbbell hang clean and jerks, and a 14 calorie row). Yes, it was a lofty goal, but if it was reasonable would it really be a goal? They only make foam fingers that say we're #1, not we're #4.

I finished the first round right around the two minute mark. If I could keep that pace for the full 20 minutes I could get through 10 rounds. Of course, if I could keep that pace for the full 20 minutes I'd also be a cyborg.

As time elapsed, reality hit, and realizing my goal of 10 rounds probably wasn't going to happen, I set a new goal of completing at least 8 rounds. This is actually something important not just in working out, but in life – creating a new goal when a previous goal becomes unattainable. There's no reason to be disappointed you didn't reach your ultimate goal when you can create smaller goals to reach for along the way.

With a little over 3 minutes left I was into my 8th round, and upon completing it I heard a voice say, "C'mon Adam, 45 seconds." It was not one of the voices in my head, it was Coach Rich pushing/rooting me on (I can only imagine what the looks would've been on the faces of all the doctors who only viewed me as a diagnosis had they been watching this scene!).

I completed the next round of knee raises, and after my third hang clean and jerk time ran out.

My total was 8 rounds + 11 reps, for a score of 267.

Week 2 – 18.2

After scaling 18.1 I initially thought I was also going to scale 18.2, which was a 1-10 rep ladder of dumbbell squats and burpee bar jumps, followed by a max weight clean.

After warming up I picked up 35 lb dumbbells and they felt … light. Still unsure I'd be able to Rx the workout, I picked up 40 lb dumbbells. Again, they felt light. So I picked up the Rx dumbbells, the 50 pounders, just to see if I could handle them. They didn't feel light, but I felt like I could probably get through a handful of rounds with them.

A year ago my big question was, "Which doctor will I be using for chemo?" My big question on this day was, "Can I Rx CrossFit Open workout 18.2?"

After doing a few dumbbell squats with the 50 lb dumbbells I decided I'd Rx 18.2, which had a 12-minute time cap.

The first couple rounds felt pretty good. After the 8th round, however, I was wiped. It was at that point I heard a voice telling me to keep pushing, telling me to get one more round in. That voice belonged to Coach Chris, as he encouraged me to keep it moving (again, doctors who viewed me as just a diagnosis, and didn't ask me any questions, were really in the dark as to my recovery capabilities. How could they have possibly told me what I would, or wouldn't, be able to do if they didn't ask what I was able to do in the first place?)

When I got to the burpee part of round 9 I had to hustle. After my 6th burpee I could hear Chris say, "Hit the floor as fast as you can!" I banged out 3 more burpees, and just as my feet hit the floor completing my 9th burpee, the clocked beeped, signifying time had expired.

I'd completed 9 rounds! I was out of breath, my legs were shaking, and I felt incredibly proud that I challenged myself to Rx 18.2.

A few days later I'd feel an even greater sense of pride when, at the behest of just about everyone, I gave 18.2 another try in an attempt to better my score.

12 minutes later I hadn't just bettered my previous score, I'd blown it out of the water, having completed all 10 rounds in 11:27, and a 138 pound power clean before the clock hit 12 (shout out to my buddy Charles for adding the extra 3 lbs before the lift)!

I looked at my score and couldn't believe it, and that exact feeling is what keeps me going. It's why I kept creating athletic goals for myself while going through surgery, chemo, and another surgery.

Not everyone's goal is going to be something of this nature. Since going through chemo I've helped some folks with their own recovery journeys, and sometimes an athletic feat is walking to the mailbox, but as I've noted to them, "You walked to the mailbox today? That's awesome! Celebrate that accomplishment. Tomorrow, see if you can walk one house further down, or one block further down, before coming back to get your mail."

I'm a huge believer in the idea that accomplishments snowball. Once you have one, you reach for another, and another, and whether it's adrenaline, or endorphins, or some science thing I'm completely unaware of, it makes you feel great because you continually see yourself succeeding.

As corny as it sounds, there really is power in positivity.

Week 3 – 18.3

As I watched the announcement of 18.3, I wasn't thrilled hearing overhead squats, and muscle ups, would be prominent parts of the workout.

I've never been great at overhead squats (although I am getting much better at them), and I've achieved one muscle up in all my time working out. Throw in the fact that I'd been completely unable to even work on these movements, and I was initially pretty bummed about 18.3.

Note, I said "initially."

After getting over the fact that all I'd be able to accomplish is the very first part of the workout, which was 100 double unders (a double under is when you get the jump rope under twice per jump), I decided to rework the rest of the workout.

Sometimes an Open workout is about absolutely killin' it. Sometimes it's about knowing your limitations, and doing what you can to work around them. This applies to a lot of things in life.

Because I teach the martial arts, I know not everyone learns at the same pace, and each individual has to work within their limitations. Can't kick high? OK, don't throw an awful kick and potentially hurt yourself, instead kick out the knee and work from there.

This was my thought process when reworking 18.3. I kept the initial 100 double unders, but substituted other movements for what I was currently unable to do. Wanting to test how far I'd come in recovery, I threw pull ups into the mix. It was the first time I'd attempted them since the surgery.

I went through two rounds of the following:

100 double unders
20 thrusters at 95 lb

50 double unders
12 pull ups
50 double unders
20 dumbbell snatches at 35 lb
50 double unders
12 pull ups

Was it actually 18.3? No. Was I able to do pull ups for the first time since my surgery in November, and work on moves that will help me eventually accomplish the moves I had to substitute for? Yes.

Instead of looking at the workout and saying, "I can't do that," I looked at the workout and said, "I can work on getting to that."

This is another important aspect of dealing with hurdles in life. Some hurdles are *really* big, and you might not be able to get over them in one leap, but hurdles in life aren't like hurdles on a track – you're allowed to build a ladder to get over your hurdles in life, and take it one step at a time until you find yourself on the other side, victorious.

In my case, I felt every round counted for something, even if they didn't necessarily count towards my Open score.

Week 4 – 18.4

Much like 18.3, the second element of 18.4 – in this case, handstand pushups – was a movement I didn't have, so I created my own an Rx/Scaled combo where I started Rx with the deadlifts, but then switched to Scaled, doing hand release pushups.

In the initial 21-15-9 WOD I made it into the round of 9, alternating Rx/Scaled, knocking out a total of 38 deadlifts at 225, and 36 hand release pushups, in the 9-minute time-cap.

My biggest takeaway from this was that my deadlifts were crawling back to what they were before my November surgery, and that excited me.

What did I say just a few paragraphs ago about building a ladder to get over a hurdle? I'd built another rung, and that's always something worth celebrating.

Week 5 – 18.5

After a fan vote, the WOD I was hoping for became our final Open WOD – thrusters (a front squat into an overhead press) and chest to bar pull ups, each ascending by 3 each round (3-6-9-12, etc.), for 7 minutes.

I showed up HYPED for this one. My ranking in my division (men ages 35-39) in the state of CT was at #248, and even though I wasn't doing the Open for the numbers aspect of it – I was doing it to prove something to myself, and others, about coming back from cancer to compete – I not-so-secretly wanted to work my way into the top 200.

After warming up, I loaded up my bar to the Rx weight of 100 lbs, and positioned it so I could do my thrusters and then simply turn around to do my pull ups. I had a plan to go unbroken for the thrusters for the first two rounds, and do the pull ups in sets of three.

Coach Rich started the clock, and my plan worked really well for the first two rounds. In round three I had to break up the thrusters, which I expected, and in round four, when it was 12 of each, I had to break them up more than I wanted to. I also started doing the pull ups in sets of one (shout out to Coach Rich for saying, "Sets of one now." The advice saved time, which is incredibly valuable in a 7-minute WOD). Then the greatest thing happened, and it's my favorite aspect of the community at my gym – I started to hear everyone encouraging me to keep going.

At the pull up bar I heard a chorus of "C'mon, Adam! One more!" and once the pull ups were complete there were a plethora of voices saying, "Get a thruster in! Ten seconds! Pick it up now!"

I picked it up. I got a thruster in. Not only that, of all the thrusters I did, it felt the strongest, and I know without that encouragement it probably wouldn't have happened.

In total, I ended up doing 61 reps, getting through the round of 12, plus that 1 thruster.

Walking out of the gym I felt a huge sense of accomplishment as my friends Rich, Sacha, and Chris ALL said my effort was impressive.

My Final Score

After five weeks of crazy workouts, pushing myself to the limit, and pretending to not care about my ranking, but actually kinda-sorta caring about my ranking, my 2018 CrossFit Open was complete.

As far as men in the state of CT age 35-39 (I was at the ancient age of 39, competing against all the whippersnappers in the division. For the next Open, I'd be a whippersnapper in the 40-44 year old division), I came pretty close to reaching my goal of finishing in the top 200. Honestly, though, what impressed me most was my progression through the weeks.

Week 1: 318
Week 2: 265
Week 3: 261
Week 4: 248
Week 5: 240

With the Open complete I presented a friendly challenge, not just to the folks in my gym, but to anyone who had been reading my posts:

With this year's Open complete, I'd like to nominate some folks to write a CrossFit Open diary NEXT year. I chose these three groups of people specifically to combat/conquer common misconceptions about working out, and because I think their Open stories would be great reads.

1. Someone over 50

Misconception to conquer – "I'm too old to work out."

I know there are quite a few amazing people at SOSF who qualify for the AARP while still kicking butt at every AMRAP (As Many Round As Possible). Show the world what ya got, and in the process, show an older generation that staying in shape, and being healthy, CAN be done.

2. A working parent

Misconception to conquer – "I don't have the time to work out."

I hear this complaint from people who DON'T have kids, so to read about someone who juggles kids, work, and doing their best in the Open would be inspiring. Plus, it could help a lot of parents with the work-life-kids balancing act.

3. A first timer

For a lot of newbies the Open can seem really daunting. I'd love to read the story of a member who decides 2019 is going to be the year they take on this challenge for the first time. Even if they scale every workout, I know there will be a number of triumphs, and reasons to celebrate, during the five-week span.

I have no idea how many people took me up on this challenge, but you'll note I mentioned specific misconceptions I wanted to see conquered. Perhaps I was thinking of all the doctors who only viewed me as a diagnosis, rather than a person.

CHAPTER 19:
WHOA, I REALLY DID THAT?

It was crazy to think about. A little under five months ago I was groggily waking up in a hospital bed after having part of a lung removed, and now I was looking at my score after completing the 2018 CrossFit Open.

Actually, if you'll allow me to indulge in some self-congratulatory behavior here – I didn't just complete the Open, I kicked some serious butt in the Open!

One of my first thoughts after seeing my results was, "I can't wait to see how I'll do next year, when I'm back at 100%!"

My mindset wasn't on taking a breather. Heck, I'd just recently spent two weeks quite literally figuring out how to breathe again. Why would I want to slow down now? I was ready for the next challenge. Of course, I was hoping it wouldn't be another medically-inspired one.

I thought about all the other people in the rankings and wondered what they might have been going through at the time, not in an egotistical "ha ha, I beat you and I was going through a major recovery" way, but in a "I have no idea what else might be going on in these people's lives, and I wonder what their scores mean to them" way.

I bet there was someone near last place who was just super stoked they'd worked their way to being healthy enough to compete, and that's pretty awesome.

Thinking about the longview of what I'd been through, in the span of roughly 14 months I'd been diagnosed with cancer, had surgery to remove a testicle, gone through chemo, earned my fifth degree black belt, had part of a lung removed, kicked butt the 2018 CrossFit Open, and I didn't miss a deadline the entire time.

In retrospect, I'd accomplished my biggest overarching goal – I'd refused to let a diagnosis define me.

Sure, I have some scars that show my path wasn't an easy one. I like to joke that I have my first date scars, and my third date scar. My first date scars are the ones from my lung surgery, and my third date scar is the one from my testicular cancer surgery.

I view all my scars as proverbial notches in my belt, and when I look at them I think about what I conquered, and the way in which I fought those battles.

Before my diagnosis I may have, at times, thought I was invincible. Ironically, after all was said and done, I came out the other side stronger than ever.

EPILOGUE

People often ask me, "How did you become so driven?"

I wish I had a simple answer for that. It probably stems from a combination of things.

First off, I'm a Type A person. Combine that with excessive amounts of caffeine, and I'm basically always one step away from being Cornholio.

Second, as an only child who is self-employed, and lives by himself (at least as of the writing of this book), if something needs to get done, I know I have to be the one to do it.

Thirdly, when it comes to being driven, what's the other option? Being a lump, and getting nothing accomplished? As you saw from how I dealt with the days immediately following my surgeries, I don't do sedentary well.

I also have a big long-term goal in life (me, having a goal? What a shock!) – when all is said and done, and I'm at an age where I constantly want the heat turned up, and get senior discounts everywhere I go, I want to be the old guy who has the most cool stories to tell.

I gotta say, I think kicking cancer's ass while training for my fifth degree black belt test qualifies as a pretty cool story, and coming back from lung surgery to compete in the CrossFit Open is a pretty cool story, as well.

Looking back on everything I went through, I learned a lot, and I have three pieces of advice for anyone who is going through something major (or even if you're going through something that doesn't qualify as catastrophic. I'm not a participant in the Struggle Olympics. Just because I had cancer doesn't mean I don't care when someone has a cold).

1. Create goals for yourself

Having the ultimate goals of earning my fifth-degree black belt, and competing in the CrossFit Open, gave me something to shoot for. Within those goals I created smaller goals, rungs on a ladder, if you will, that helped me get to my ultimate goals.

I found that reaching each smaller goal creates a feeling of accomplishment, which acts as inspiration to continue working towards the next goal.

2. Recognize all your accomplishments, no matter how small, and allow them to snowball

Some days we feel like we can take on the world. On other days we feel like we can barely get out of bed. For the days that qualify as the latter it's especially important to recognize smaller accomplishments, because in reality, on a day when you feel like you can't get out of bed – like the day after my first surgery when it literally took me over half a dozen attempts to get out of bed – small accomplishments are actually a very big deal.

Did you get out of bed? That's an accomplishment!

Brush your teeth? Accomplishment!

Make breakfast? Accomplishment!

If you've accomplished all that, and it isn't even 9am, what else can you accomplish in a day when you weren't sure you'd even make it out of bed?

We do a lot over the course of a day, and recognizing this on our toughest of days can create a real confidence boost.

3. If you're going through something – whether it's physical, mental, or emotional – tell your friends and family about it

Far too many of us suffer in silence because we either think our problems aren't big enough to talk about, or we don't want to bother our friends with what we're going through. I'm here to tell you – don't keep your problems to yourself!

My friends are the reason the "Stay Strong and Have Faith" bracelets exist, and have made their way around the world.

As you know, I had to come to terms with asking my friends for help. It's something I'm still not great at, but we ALL need help at some point in life. During my down times, my friends were there to pick me up – whether in person, or online – but it was only because I was open with them about what I was going through that they could be there for me.

Asking for help isn't a sign of weakness, it's a sign of humanity.

Speaking of humanity, another huge lesson I came away with from all of this is that humanity is something we all have in common. No matter which sports team you root for, religion you practice, gender you're attracted to, political party you align yourself with, or place that you're from, we all come together when a friend needs us.

With that in mind, maybe, just maybe, we should stop shouting at each other whenever we have a disagreement. Let's take a breath, find our commonalities, and work from there.

My journey has also led me to learn more than I ever wanted to know about doctors, and choosing the right ones.

If there are any doctors reading this – please ask your patients questions about their lives. We are more than just a set of X-rays, CAT Scans, and blood tests. We have lives, lives that matter very much to us, and one 40-year-old male's life is often completely different from the next. By asking us questions you'll have a better handle on what we're about, what we expect out of life, and how we'll deal with whatever we have to go through. You'll know if you should be pushing us harder, or holding us back. You'll also be surprised at how much better your professional advice is taken after you simply ask us a question or two about who we are. Those questions, even more than all the diplomas and honors on your office walls, make us feel we're in good hands, because they show you care.

If you're a patient, and you're looking for a doctor, please remember you don't have to work with the first one you meet. Unless you have something that needs to be dealt with immediately, make as many visits to different doctors as necessary to find one you trust, get along with, and who understands your goals. You're going to be seeing your doctor often, so you really want the right one for you.

Being that goals have been a common theme throughout these pages, you might be wondering what my goals are for this book.

My fun goal is to be a guest on all the talk shows I watched while I was in chemo. I want the nurses to be able to say, "That guy there, on the TV right now, he was in one of these chairs. If he can make it out, you can, too!"

My second goal was exemplified perfectly in a tweet by my friend Jake Palumbo of SpaceLAB Recordings

"The manner in which you quietly tied the Rambo bandana around your head, & hit cancer with roundhouse kicks until it said 'I don't want any more trouble' reminds me to not give up at certain challenges more often than you might think."

Simply put, I want to inspire people.

As you know, during my cancer journey I wrestled with the word "inspiration," but in the end I realized being called an inspiration was one of the coolest things in the world, because me living my life was in some small way, shape, or form, pushing others forward, as well.

That's my ultimate goal for this book.

Thank you for reading my story. I hope you now feel inspired to take on any challenge that may come your way.

ACKNOWLEDGMENTS

I was considering not writing an acknowledgments page for fear of forgetting people, and then having to deal with feeling uncomfortable every time I bumped into one of those people. I still have that concern, but I'm gonna give it a go.

First and foremost, I have to thank my parents, because if I don't, they won't let me come over to their house, eat their food, and play with their cat. OK, it's really because they had my back through all of this, and never wavered in their confidence in my ability to kick cancer's ass on my own terms. I love you both very much.

It goes without saying that I have a ton of love and respect for the doctors and nurses who helped me get through this, and occasionally (OK, often) looked at me like I was crazy. This includes Dr. Duda, Dr. Kingsly, Dr. Ebright (and nurse Lauren), Dr. Simkovitz, Dr. Dowling, and Dr. Funt, as well as my chemo nurses – Nancy, Melissa, Megan, Mallory, and Katlyn. You are all amazing, and I appreciate you.

A huge shout out goes to my extended families at SOSF CrossFit and Chiropractic, and Fred Villari's Studio Of Self Defense of Fairfield, CT. You helped me train through the pain, achieve my goals, and with the exception of some required tweaking of workouts, treated me no differently than normal. I appreciate you all more than you can possibly know.

Another huge shout out goes to my music industry people. I'm sure you've probably heard talk of how people in the music industry are shady, but the fact of the matter is I had a heck of a lot of support from everyone I work with – artists, publicists, editors, etc. I know the music industry has some bad folks in it, but the hundreds of people I have around me – on both the music side, and journalistic side – are damned good people, and I appreciate them.

To my friends who were able to visit me – thank you. I appreciate you making the effort to come by, chill out, bring food, and in one case, supply some … let's call them herbal supplements.

Anthony Gargano, even though I mentioned you by name in the book I have to shout you out again here. You made sure I would not be shaving my head alone, you made the "Stay Strong and Have Faith" bracelets, and you and your entire family have always been incredible to me. While I'm at it, I should also shout out our entire fantasy baseball league. I have no idea how I survived that draft. Actually, yes I do – by drafting a terrible team (and no, I don't do that every year)!

To everyone who wore a "Stay Strong and Have Faith" bracelet – thank you. Your support was not only noticed, it continually gave me an incredible boost that no drug could replicate.

My social media friends also played a big role in all of this. Seeing your continued support on a daily basis was awesome. Your "likes" were more powerful than you could ever imagine. I appreciate all of you!

I also want to give a gigantic shout out to Kristi King-Morgan and the entire Dreaming Big

Publications team – especially my editor, Alexander Crawford, who was fantastic to work with. Thank you for believing in my vision, and making *ChemBro* a reality.

Finally, one last great big thank you I want to hand out is to YOU! Thank you for reading *ChemBro*. You rock! Now get out there and climb a mountain!

(You know that was a metaphor, right? I don't expect all of you to climb mountains … unless that's your thing, in which case, go for it!)

ABOUT THE AUTHOR

Adam Bernard is a music industry veteran, lifelong martial artist, and general lifter of heavy things, who has been working in media since 2000. He's old school enough to have written a newspaper column, be one of the original music bloggers, and pen 14 national magazine cover stories along the way.

If you live in the NYC area, you've probably seen him at a show.

He prefers his music venues intimate, his whiskey on the rocks, and his baseball played without the DH.

He is still waiting for Vanessa Hudgens to reply to one of his tweets. (If you're reading this, Vanessa, I'm @AdamsWorldBlog)